SUCH A NICE GUY

BY
PHIL TORCIVIA

Illustrated by Rebecca Shockley

Copy editing by Linda M. Au

Copyright © 2009 Phil Torcivia
All rights reserved.

ISBN: 1-4392-5529-6
ISBN-13: 9781439255292

Visit www.booksurge.com to order additional copies.

Table of Contents

Dedication vii
Acknowledgment...ix
Introduction xi
Phil & Testes Plus 500,000,000 1
The Walk of Shame..5
Potty Mouth 7
The Bad Boy... 11
The Irresistible Pull of the Ex 15
Proper Care for Your Pet Phil 19
Blinders 23
How to End a Friendship... 27
No More Excuses.. 31
I Want You Walking Away from Me....................................... 35
She Wants Me 39
If You Love Him, Leave for Him 43
How Do I Work You?.. 47
The Gatekeeper.. 51
How Single Are You? 55
Think Ink 59
Corporate Holiday Parties Suck... 61
Be Nice and Lie to Me 65
Uninvited... 69

Black Specks in the Diamond	73
The Perfect Kiss	77
Random Things about Me	81
Carlsbad Cougar Runs from Atheist	83
Tag, I'm It	87
She Said She Was Happy, Very Sadly	91
Trying on Shoes	95
Three Things	99
The Committed Should Be Committed	103
Hot for Teacher	107
What Are You On?	111
Grumpy Old Man	115
The Cougar	119
Home Field Advantage	123
Net Mating Benefit	127
Yes or No	131
Hot Mess	137
What to Wear	139
Battle of the Minds	143
Expectations	147
Happy Anniversary to Me	151
Married Women	155
Home Wrecker	159
Letter to Myself	163
Battle of the Genders	167
The Lover You Won't Fall in Love With	171
Bathroom Etiquette	175
Speed Dating 101	179
Why I Sleep Alone	183

Things That Make Me Angry 187
Conversations with My Little Friend at a Wine Bar 193
No Offense 197
Scavenger Women 201
Baggage 205
Noassatol: The Next Pandemic 211
Instant Entertainer, Just Add Alcohol 215
Hair 219
First Impressions 223
Internet Mating 227
The Come On 231
How I Love Chrissy Russo 235
Aging 239
Tell Me a Story 241
Professing 245
I'll Treat You 249
The Real Housewives of Phil's House 253
Speech Template for the Next Governor
    Caught Cheating 257
More Than Just a Haircut 261
Friends I Should Leave Home 265
The Smothering 269
Del Martians 273
The Marriage Lease 277
The Turtle Always Wins 281
Bite Me 285
Rules for Men at the Gym 289
Barriers 293
Ex Games 297

The Chase	301
All Ears	305
Office Olympics	309
Pockets	313
Puddles	317
Sounds That Hurt	321
Nuts and Bolts	325
Temptation	329
Such a Nice Guy	333

Dedication

For my mother, Dolores, who sacrificed a lucrative career to provide her loving care, nurturing more than her share of children. I'm fortunate to have your encouragement, support, and tolerance.

For Pop, known to his friends as "Chet Who?" The most generous person I have ever met, he served his country and accumulated friends and free drink cups everywhere he went. Thank you for your work ethic, discipline, and fantastic sense of humor.

Acknowledgment

This book goes out to all my friends and family who kept saying, "Dude, you need to write a book." This is entirely your fault.

Introduction

Who am I? What do I know? What qualifications do I have to observe and evaluate?

I'm just a man in his late forties who was fortunate enough to have a relatively baggage-free second shot at love and a sense of humor to avoid the depression that comes with rejection. I'm also lucky to be able to work from home, giving me the time to reflect and write about love on the West Coast. Finally, yes it's true: people in Southern California enjoy nicer weather and provide a large dose of physical and social dysfunction, giving me plenty of writing material.

This is not an autobiography. I embellish most of what I write to make it entertaining. Life is interesting, but to embellish is to add spice to the meat of a story. Forgive me for exaggerating and being judgmental and shallow at times. A nice, predictable, and politically correct Phil is a boring Phil—in person and in print. That's why I drink, and that's why I use my imagination.

Some people will find an essay or two they are convinced is about them. Rest assured that nothing in this book is about you, it's all about me: such a nice guy.

Phil & Testes Plus 500,000,000

You think the Gosselins have it tough? Bah. I have millions of little ones to worry about. Imagine taking care of such a brood. Sure, they are tiny and spend most of their days swimming, but I'm exhausted trying to keep up with them. There's keeping them safe, feeding, and taking them out to play, just to name a few of the draining activities.

I take my children with me everywhere I go, even to the gym. Although Daddy loves the stationary bike and sauna, my little ones are none too impressed. I tell them a happy daddy is the best daddy so sometimes they need to suck it up and take one for the team. If Daddy stops working out then they will not get to spend as much time doing their favorite activity: egg hunting. Oh, my boys can't get enough of that. They don't want one Easter a year either. Nope, not my boys. Every weekend is Easter in their minds. Good Friday? Every Friday.

I have to be careful when I drink alcohol because I sometimes neglect my children, and they beg me to come out and play. Nag, nag, nag. They start looking for eggs where there are few to be found. Sometimes Daddy meets a nice woman his age. You'd think the boys would be happy. Nope. I explain (in my baby voice) that older women have more experience with them and are more fun to play with. Yet, when the boys get involved, they whine and complain that she doesn't play nice. Her eggs are too hard to find.

My children are always up before I am in the morning. God, what I would give to be able to sleep in. Sometimes I take them out to play right before bedtime, hoping to tire them out. They love to watch TV, but Daddy loves sports, and they have no interest. We end up watching their favorite shows as I try to tire them out, but still in the morning it's "We're up, Daddy, get up!" and no more sleep for me. I tell them I have to pee, but they won't let me. They want to play first. How exhausting.

A few years back I was concerned that my boys were dysfunctional or had A.D.D. I was married and putting my boys to work doing regular egg hunts. They sucked at it, so off to the doctor's office we went. They sent us to the "collection room" where I was told to get my boys out so they could be examined, counted, and evaluated. They were a little shy to come out, but we found some of their favorite magazines (which Daddy held with his sleeve, not his skin, because the pages were wrinkled and gross). After a bit of coaxing, they finally did come out. I felt bad because I hardly had time to name all 500,000,000 of them. It turned out that there were some slow ones and even a few two-headed little monsters, but most of them were healthy and good swimmers. Daddy was so proud.

Well, I wish I had the time to tell you more. They're up again and nagging me about going out for another egg hunt tonight. I told them Daddy's tired, and if they keep it up, he'll have to hire them a playmate. They're oddly OK with that. I threatened to take them to the shower. They hate showers. However, Daddy taught them how to make pretend, so they stop nagging him. I'm sorry, I have to go … Phil the 216,549th is crying and wants his pacifier (*nookie*).

The Walk of Shame

I define this as the walk a woman takes from a man's residence to her car after a night of bumping nasties. Did this originate with the "Bridge of Sighs" in Venice? I sure hope not. After all, it doesn't come with a prison sentence.

SUCH A NICE GUY

I find this walk hurtful (*sniff*) and I demand an apology on behalf of my scorned brothers.

Why is the walk shameful?

- If the neighbors see you, they will think you're slutty.
- You're wearing the same clothes from last night (with an assortment of new pulls, wrinkles, and stains).
- Your sobriety has exposed my flaws.

When I leave a girl's house, I take the "walk of pride" because:

- If the neighbors see me, they will think I'm stud-worthy, trustworthy, and responsible for all those funny noises they heard last night (except the sirens, usually).
- My wearing the same clothes makes them more weathered looking, which is fashionable for dudes.
- You're beautiful and my leaving after sunrise proves you're not a vampire.

I will submit a Proposition P to have it renamed the "walk of pride" in the next election. In the meantime, you can park closer, leave before sunrise, dress like a meter maid, or drive a UPS truck.

Potty Mouth

Maybe I was married while this trend developed and never had the opportunity to delve into the seemingly popular world of dirty talk. This is completely new to me. I'm not going to judge it because frankly I'm not qualified. I can't see any harm in words between consenting adults so why my discomfort? Does this stem from unfamiliarity or am I missing the potty mouth gene? Was I traumatized as a youth? Maybe Ivory soap was on my menu far too often in my youth.

I discovered this phenomenon within the first few weeks of migrating to the western dating scene. Internet dating brought me a unique young woman I'll describe as five feet of Gothic goodness: black hair and clothing, pale skin, and a whole new (to me) level of sex drive.

She asked me on our first date what I thought of porn. I detected a setup, so I answered neutrally: "I've seen it, why?" Her response was unanticipated.

"Because I find it a huge turn-on," she said matter-of-factly. That triggered a wide range of mental (and some physical) reactions.

- Score! I think I can bypass the dinner, flowers, and movie rituals.
- OMG, she's a ho. (That's my feline feminine side.)
- How am I going to measure up to her favorite actors? (Not well.)
- She's testing me. She wants me to confess to being a pervert.
- How can I keep a straight face and not lose this romantic moment?
- Family Christmas dinner is going to be an interesting one this year.

Much later in our budding relationship (the next night), we were making out, and she whispered in my ear, "Are you into dirty talk?" I had similar reactions to those above. I started thinking I must have missed the memo while I was out of the dating pool. Was I too prudish?

I didn't know how to respond so I stuttered, "Umm, well, I don't know, but I guess …" which she interrupted by shushing me with her finger over my lips. I mumbled through her fingers, "How dirty?"

"Tell me what you're going to do to my dirty little [insert the atom bomb of all naughty words here]," she said with raised eyebrow. I couldn't help it. I laughed. Ah rats, Gothic goodness gone for good.

When I confessed this to a close friend, he didn't have the shocked reaction I expected. He said, "And so, what did you do to it?"

"Dude, she said the 'c' word! Are you kidding me? That would have gotten me a month on the couch when I was married," I pleaded, looking for sympathy, to no avail.

Here are some other popular literary gems I'm learning:

- "Who's your daddy?" (That one I don't get. Like a girl wants to be thinking of her father now?)
- "Yeah, you like that, don't you?" (Must be an *American Idol* thing.)
- "You make me so [insert flattering adjective]." (Whom is it flattering?)

Back to my studies. I have so much to learn. Every time I'm with a nice girl I flinch, worrying that one of those verbal missiles is coming my way. I'm not prepared to respond properly. Maybe a foreign language would work? Nothing I say would be understood so ole potty pie-hole can hear anything she wants. *¿Cómo brillante soy?*

The Bad Boy

He's broke, he has baggage, and he has more tattoos than manners. His psycho ex stalks him, he won't wear a condom, and he's too old/young for you. He drinks himself blind and then wants to fool around, he smells, and he flirts with other women right in front of you. He grabs your butt (even in church), he thinks Pinot means incontinence, and he swears at the TV. His dog sheds on you, his laundry pile has become a new life form, his fingernails are sprouting weeds, and his toenails look like Fritos. He sprays antiperspirant on his nether region, he eats leftover burritos with syrup for breakfast with a warm Bud Light, and best of all: *you love him*!

I'm a far cry from a "bad boy," in fact, I doubt I could act like one. I know, for some reason, women like that man though, and if I tried to pull it off, they'd see right through it. The best "good boys" can do is wear T-shirts that look like tattoos because we're too scared to get one. Actually, it isn't fear for me; I know how quickly I get bored with the same *hat* let alone permanent skin pigment. Maybe I'll go unshaven for a day; scruff means rough, right?

So what's the big draw anyway? Are women looking to cage and tame the lion? Is he a science project? I don't think that's it because once you clean him up he'll be a boring "good boy." Is it a social thing? Do your girlfriends admire your unkempt ape-man more than your Fendi? His public displays of affection draw wrinkled noses from the sisters but deep inside, they are saying, "Yes, you grab that, you dirty boy."

It is funny how much "turn a good boy into bad boy" merchandise is out there. Besides the tattoo T-shirts, there are torn jeans, worn leather boots, silver rings, earrings, trucker hats, pickup trucks, motorcycles, chewing tobacco, large dogs, 24-ounce beers, and UFC fights. Is that what it takes? Really?

It seems you girls only like pretty boys if they're gay. Oh, you'll compliment a nice shirt, say my cologne smells nice, and admire my watch. Meanwhile you have an eye on the Tommy Lee Wannabe.

I demand an explanation on behalf of all straight men who read (books, not the sports section), shower daily, iron, wear cologne, and trim our nails with a clipper, not our teeth. Fess up or I swear I will get a skull tattoo ... then again, my arm hair would make that look as ridiculous as driving a Harley.

Ugh, I give up. Pass the Pinot.

The Irresistible Pull of the Ex

I got into an interesting discussion recently. It started with my friend's embarrassing admission that he relented and returned to the woman he had recently scorned. There was a young woman involved in the discussion, which began with a relentless beating of the confessor. It was nice to hear both the male and female takes on the matter at hand.

From his perspective, the relationship was mostly physical. He described his older woman as overbearing, immature, and superficial (but worth putting up with). When they split he told us, "She's insane, I can't believe it lasted this long."

When he returned to her, our predictable male response was, "Of course you did."

The girl that was present was appalled. From her perspective, since he constantly complained about his girl, it is unfathomable that he would ever return to such torture. She was disgusted, but we understood. You may ask how that could be. Well, there is a perfectly logical explanation for it.

When he latched onto the woman, it was obvious to us men that he was doing it for physical reasons. Now, you can't expect a guy to give any such impression to female acquaintances. If he did, the girls would consider him slutty, superficial, and primitive and thus remove themselves from future consideration. He should have expected that once reality sets in, the parts he loved would come with parts sometimes not so much.

On the other hand, if he bragged about his relationship by saying how intellectually stimulating their conversations are, how eagerly he awaits those hand-in-hand romantic strolls along the beach, and how he loves making dinner together, we would throw drink garnishes at him and revoke his men's club membership.

He brags about the physical parts of his relationship to his male friends. I'll keep this PG and not give gory details, but you get the picture. With women (and only the attractive ones) he discusses the challenges of their intellectual relationship, and mentions exactly nothing about the physical part. In fact, he minimizes or twists things in a way that makes him sound stud-worthy. He also gives women the impression that he's on the way out, keeping his options open.

There you have it. I apologize, men, if I have exposed our strategy, but I bet the fairer sex is onto us anyway. We're not as smart as we think we are, so it's safer to just shrug and admit, "Exes need love too."

Proper Care for Your Pet Phil

1. There's no biting of the Phil. Nope, never, no place ever.
2. The punching of the Phil is prohibited.
3. Spanking of the Phil is acceptable when gentle and through clothing.

4. Do not, under any circumstance, vomit near the Phil.
5. If you must kiss the Phil, please avoid choking him with your tongue.
6. In case #1 isn't clear, it includes goatee, shoulder, neck, lower lip, and ears.
7. There's no putting anything wet into the Phil's ear.
8. The Phil's rear is exit-only no matter what your ex liked.
9. Please, handle the Phil's family jewels gently.
10. There's no snoring near the Phil.
11. Under no circumstance is your dog allowed to shed or drool on the Phil.
12. Avoid the Phil's belly-button.
13. The Phil is not interested in your ex-boyfriend, spouse, or boss.
14. Do not attempt to bring the Phil to church.
15. There's no trying to feed the Phil meat, except breastuses.
16. If you must watch the Phil play baseball, pay attention and avoid the Phil's perverted teammates.
17. You are never to call the Phil "baby," ever.
18. The Phil is not interested in a threesome, unless you have a twin.
19. Don't try to make out in public with the Phil; it gives him anxiety.
20. Phils don't do camping, yoga, or salsa dancing.
21. Don't introduce the Phil to your horny friends, unless you want to share him.
22. Never assume that a single Phil implies a dysfunctional Phil.

23. The Phil is not your website designer.
24. Never compliment the Phil by asking who decorates and cleans his house.
25. Don't look in the Phil's bedside table.
26. Stop trying to groom and dress the Phil.
27. There's no making the Phil do body shots of tequila if he has to drive.
28. Do not place dark chocolate near the Phil.
29. No, the Phil has not slept with any bartenders (not for lack of trying).
30. There's no weeping to the Phil.

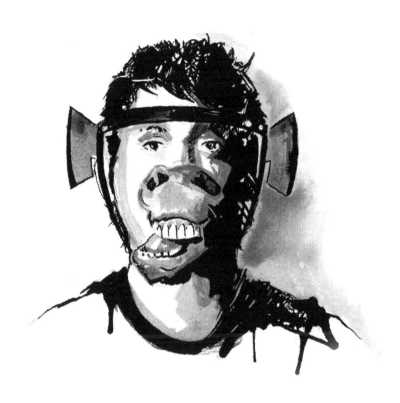

Blinders

    This is not a disease. I was made this way, like most men. Is it strictly evolutionary: bioLOGICal? Why can't I avoid the cleavage? Frontal or rear. If there's a valley, I have to look. I don't want to, I understand it's disrespectful if I'm with a date (unless she's the target), and I've gotten enough "I'm up here" return looks to learn my lesson. I can't help it, damn it.

I was with a date recently and in close quarters at the noon position was one (or two) of my favorite things about fall out. It gets a wee bit chilly in the evenings this time of year (East Coasters would beg to differ, but I have been spoiled). Girls break out the clingy sweaters that are so warm and inviting. The target had on a button-down, buttoned up to barely cover the twin peaks.

Why can't I just glance, acknowledge, and walk away? Every time I looked, they were there saying, "Ahem, see me, appreciate me, and don't you stare for more than two seconds." Is that cumulative, or per glance? I think I topped twenty seconds cumulative, so cuff me, Officer.

Come on, they are just globs of fat anyway, what's the big draw? My mind kept saying, "Quit it, she's with a date, so are you, look away." My evil instincts kept encouraging me to find a reason to glance that way. "Oh, the sunset." "What a nice painting." "I never noticed the quality furniture here." I'm sure my date was on to me. I tried the people-watching excuse and got the well-deserved raised eyebrow from her.

It's the same with low-cut jeans having an inch of skin above the seam and a piece of lace peaking over the top. That's even more of a draw because the target usually can't detect my ogling. I say *usually* because I have learned to beware of mirrors (especially at the gym) and evil friends willing to throw my childish butt under the bus.

How do I cure this? Do I wear my sunglasses at night, Corey Hart? I know, just stare at my own date's boobs, right? But I've seen those already. I know it sounds immature but how many times can you watch reruns (excluding *Sex and the City* and *Ferris Bueller's Day Off*)? Just because I see skin, doesn't mean I need to touch it.

You look too. How do women get away with it?

How to End a Friendship

Do you have close friends you're sexually attracted to? Of course you do. Have you been tempted to see what would happen, if you *went there*? Of course you have. Have you ever *gone there*? Of course you have. So, are you still close friends? You liar!

This is definitely different between men and women. I've had it happen a few times (that I will admit to) since my first kiss on my neighbor's porch at age twelve. Men rarely have close girl friends that we have no desire to sleep with. I know, that sucks and we're shallow, blah blah blah. I am not my maker, so blame my ancestors.

Women maintain male friends that they wouldn't dream of sleeping with. There may be some rare male friends who they *would* sleep with. Regardless, women are better at resisting the temptation. Women can appreciate friends who will listen, be supportive, and give them honest opinions, even if those friends have more hair on their backs than their heads.

It's different for men. If you're not attractive to us, then, unless you're a close relative (red states excluded) you're not a close friend. Don't believe me? Look around. I have to admit I have some sexy female friends. I won't be sleeping with most of them—*not* because I'm not attracted to them—because I don't want to lose them as friends. Face it, most of our physical relationships end up in no relationship.

Do some introspection if you deny it. How many people have you slept with and returned to being just friends? Very few. All of your physical relationships have ended except your most recent one, if you even have one. Therefore, you're either at a 100 percent failure rate or close to it. Actually, I shouldn't call it *failure*. The relationship served a purpose so it didn't really *fail*, did it? The rub is that the purpose it served for one person was probably different for the other.

So, what should we do with a close friend that we are sexually attracted to? Stressful, huh? It's worse when you add alcohol, a recent breakup, a long marriage gone boring, and other inhibition removers. Hey, friendship is a great thing to have in a complete (with sex) relationship. Our history of physical relationship failures makes it difficult to go there. How would we recover and maintain the friendship after the physical part is over?

No More Excuses

My gender, ethnicity, religious beliefs, height, weight, and age are irrelevant. What matters is what I do, not what I look like or believe. Sorry, Mr. President. I admire you and am happy to see you earn your well-deserved place in history, but if you truly believe that discrimination will ever go away, you are deluded. It serves a purpose in life. Not always a noble one, but if you look closely it makes sense.

We, as humans, have this built-in "shortcut" that allows us to make quick decisions. Back in the tribal days, it was an even more important trait to determine a friend or foe. We make snap judgments based on appearance and related experiences. If we didn't have this ability (not flaw), we would be stuck in analysis paralysis. It's subjective but in aggregate, the judgment based on appearance is more often correct, or it wouldn't survive.

Let's look at some examples as they apply to dating and mating.

If I see a girl at the gym wearing eyeliner, revealing clothing, and spending lots of time on the inner-thigh machine, I'll assume she is single and looking. If she has on a hat, sweats, and headphones, I assume she is not at the gym for social reasons. Now, this does not apply 100 percent of the time. It's not always safe to assume, any more than assuming someone knocking at my door midmorning is trying to bring me to Jesus. Even so, it is likely, right?

Conversely, if you see a man at the gym—regardless of what he is wearing—he's seeking visual stimulation with his workout. How many all-male (non-homosexual) gyms are there? Men are often oblivious to the fact that more skin is not better from the women's perspective. There are too many older men at my gym in wife-beaters.

How about some other common—and often incorrect—interpretations?

- Tattoos—On a woman means she's promiscuous; on a man means he can kick my ass.

- Blond Hair—On a woman means she wants attention; on a man means he's a surfer dude.
- Tall—On a woman foretells uncomfortable cuddling and intimidation; on a man implies a big unit.
- Martini Up, Drinking from Straws—With a woman means she's sassy, beware of the cat; with a man shows he has a sense of security, sensitive teeth, or he's new to drinking.
- Underwear showing—On a woman means all hands on deck; on a man shows teenage immaturity.
- BMW—With a woman means she's classy and successful; with a man means he's preppy and pretentious.
- Lip Gloss—On a woman means certain oral talents are likely; on a man means the lucky fellow kissed a talented woman recently.
- Dogs—With a woman means a cold black nose in bed; on a man means … well, that depends on the dog's breed and name (which should never be poodle and Pookie).
- Drinking from a Beer Bottle—A woman doing this implies that she loves sports and is aggressive, not dainty; a man doing this implies that he farts a lot.

You get the point. I didn't go into the more sensitive areas because future employers will already raise eyebrows at my filter-free mind, and I don't want to be unemployable because of my book. Hey, if Obama can be president maybe there is hope that knowing—not seeing—is believing.

I Want You Walking Away from Me

Why do we torture ourselves in relationships by wanting the mates that require the most work? We love a challenge, don't we? Since we know all the stress it causes, is it worthwhile? I'm not referring to people that we have completely no shot at. There has to be the tiniest of openings, and then we often become obsessed with winning them over. Ironically, once we win them over, we lose interest.

It must be our competitive nature. The things that are the scarcest and that we need to work the hardest for are typically in the highest demand. We just ignore the flaws and the reasons why the wanted item is *unwanted* in the first place. If the item is barely within our reach, we want it bad. If it has flaws, no problem, we can fix those. If someone else has the item, and we think we deserve it more, we'll find a way to take it. It's so childish, isn't it?

A woman vented to me recently about her challenging relationship. She describes it as "complicated." She admits to liking the man, regardless of unspecified flaws, and she gave plenty of the usual reasons why she likes him.

- We get along.
- We agree on many things.
- We're friends.
- We talk all the time.
- We have a great sex life. (OK, she didn't say that, but I heard it.)

So what's so complicated? Well, enter the ex-girlfriend. It seems our boy has a little "cake-and-eat-it-too" strategy, which he ingeniously—but I would bet unconsciously—is using to his advantage by making it known. You can't blame him. He just has a little insurance because if the new girl doesn't work out, he'll have Old Faithful to fall back on. He may also be sensing some angst with the new girl, so he brilliantly makes himself *scarce* to increase demand.

If our boy keeps his uncertainty about his ex silent, he becomes more available and less work. Instead, he makes it known that he has some straggling feelings for the ex and wants to make sure before moving on. This drives his new girl crazy. It is masterful manipulation at its best, and I'm not sure he's doing it intentionally.

This method works and there are plenty of examples.

- When offered a job, if I say I have to wait on another offer before accepting, I can usually get a better deal.
- See the latest iPhone, Elmo, Cabbage Patch Kids, and car dealers ("This is the last one on the lot!") for retail examples.
- Put three donuts in a meeting of four people and someone goes hungry. Put five there and somebody won't want one.

How do we protect ourselves? We can play the game too, for one thing. The woman above could have said, "Fine, go meet up with your ex and work it out, but I'll be out shopping for a better man while you're gone." She could also withhold the physical goodies (the easiest way to manipulate men, and we have no defense for it). She might recognize his strategy and resist the temptation to play along. She must decide if she can live with his indecision because she's not going to change him and will frustrate herself trying.

It is complicated, but it doesn't have to be. Be aware of your desires. Do some introspection: "Why is this driving me nuts?" Sleep on it, if necessary, and most of all, demand higher quality.

She Wants Me

Nothing is as inflated and humorous as a man's ego. It serves us well most of the time, but sometimes I can't help but say, "Man, what was I/he thinking?" The competitive part of men pushes us toward pointing and laughing when a brother falls. There are also times when the crash and burn makes me cringe; I feel the pain.

I visited a local establishment (OK, a bar, that's where the stories are) and witnessed a complete unraveling of my brethren. Connected to a hotel, the bar is full of business travelers and often becomes a minefield of humor.

I'm going to surmise the man involved flew in to interview for a pharmaceutical sales position. Unbeknownst to him, people here are just plain friendlier than back east. Maybe it's the weather. But not everyone who smiles at you wants to sleep with you.

Enter two of southern California's finest women during a thirtieth birthday celebration. Even the bartender gets into the act. He has fashionable eyeglasses that he loves to remove and clean in front of the girls, so they can see and comment on his eyes. I can't criticize him; it works more often than not. "Oh you have such nice eyes, you should wear contacts," they often remark.

Anyway, they sit beside the East Coast dude: mid-thirties, button-down short-sleeve shirt tucked in Wranglers too short to hide his argyles. The girls are giddy and on wine number three or four, at minimum. They're giving all the usual mating calls (I know they aren't always mating calls, but indulge me) by flipping their hair, leaning forward to expose skin, and giggling playfully. Poor Tex Wrangler is hooked and frothing.

The one girl can't help but notice his drool and she offers up the West Coast innocent line, "Hey, how ya doin'?" For some reason he heard something completely different. I just happened to be visiting the little boys' room as he walked in, on his cell phone.

"Dude, I love it out here. You wouldn't believe it. I'm sitting at the bar and two hot chicks come in, and it's the one girl's birthday or something. They're hot, I mean smoking hot, and they're coming on to me big time, both of them. This is a sign from God, man, I'm telling you. They both want to do me! This is awesome. Seriously, they are supermodel hot and just begging for it."

I wanted to slap reality back into him. Naturally, he spent the remaining thirty minutes they stayed staring into the closest girl's back as she couldn't bear to face him. Yet, I'm sure he had his threesome, if you count his two hands. His friends from back east will never know ... but I do.

If You Love Him, Leave for Him

Many relationships simply run their course. They are hot and heavy in the beginning, exciting as the physical part develops, a struggle to find ways to keep the original intensity, frustrating as we can't, and tempting to find that fire again elsewhere.

This mostly applies to marriage. I think people stay together too long for the wrong reasons. Some of those reasons include:

- I'm staying for the kids.
- There's nothing better out there.
- It would be too expensive to leave.
- It isn't *that* bad.
- I don't care if the sex stinks. I can take care of myself.
- She or he will change.
- We'll get it back.
- I'm not happy but I'm staying for my spouse because they are happy.

Here's my solution (and don't ever hire me as a marriage counselor): you loved the person enough to enter in the relationship; now love them enough to move on. There will be anxiety and yes, your kids, family, and friends will judge you. Even so, it's your life and your first responsibility should be to yourself. If you make yourself happy (I sound like Deepak now, yuck, sorry), your loved ones will be happy for you and will enjoy your company a whole lot more.

"How will the kids cope?" Well, depending on their ages it will no doubt be different. The problem with kids is that they have limited information to go on and little experience in the relationship business. You can't expect them to understand why those funny noises coming out of the bedroom were replaced by whispered screams of anger. Yet, since they are kids, they will get over it quickly as they have their own lives to live. If Mommy and Daddy can at least be civil, they'll be able to deal with it. Better yet, if Mommy and Daddy maintain the friendship, they set a *great* example for the kids; love does not need to end in hate.

The sex thing comes up a lot. I meet women who confess that the husband doesn't seem interested in them anymore physically. Ladies, I'm here to tell you, if your man does not want to get busy with you on a regular basis, and he has no medical reasons ... *run away*! You deserve better. Sure, there are special circumstances. Sometimes people become less physically or emotionally attractive for some unexplainable reason. However, it is *real*, and *real hard* to get it back once the attraction is gone.

I recall meeting a woman in her forties. She had two kids, married for seventeen years, and was with the same man for twenty years. There was fire in her eyes when she spoke to me and looked at other available men around her. She bravely confessed within fifteen minutes of meeting me that her husband doesn't want to touch her anymore, and all the physical reasons that I could think of did not apply. She was beautiful. I wasn't sure what to tell her. "You are super hot, girlfriend, so whatever problem there is, it must be *his* problem."

She said she was seeing a counselor and that her husband was aware of it, but he refused to attend with her. That's another reason to let him go. If your mate doesn't have enough respect for you and doesn't value your relationship enough to do a painless thing like talk about it, then *you need to demand better*.

If you feel that your relationship is failing, it is. It also is failing from your mate's perspective, even if they won't admit it. It takes two happy people to make a successful relationship (OK, sometimes three, but only on TV). If you have the urge to relive the excitement of those first four weeks of your relationship, then so does your mate. What do you think the odds are that you'll find that spark again in your current relationship versus with the next lover? The house always wins so play the odds, my dear.

Making you happy is your job.

How Do I Work You?

I know, I know: "Men never read the instructions or ask for directions." Well, damn it, I'm asking. How do women work? I'm tired of guessing. I've tried all of the tab "A," slot "B," a little WD40 (vodka), twist here, and tug there methods. The levers and buttons don't work the same on all of you.

Men are primitive beasts—visual and impatient, especially at my age. So, when we meet, kindly hand us your instruction manual. Is that too much to ask?

"Oh, but the learning about each other, the experimenting, those awkward moments; it's all so exciting." I'll tell you what it is: *frustrating*. It's like trying to assemble a ten-speed bike with a stripped screwdriver and without cold beer.

It would be a lot easier if women all worked the same—not even close. This one likes to talk dirty; that one calls it a "wee wee." This one likes the cashmere sweater gift; that one is offended that I bought a size five because she's "a four even on a fat day" (like I have a decoder ring to figure out women's sizes). This one appreciates the perfume I picked out; this one takes it as a hint that she smells bad. I feel like I'm at the roulette table.

Here's how simple it could be. In your instruction manual, you list:

- Clothing and shoe sizes and designer and store preferences (please don't say Saks);
- Ring size (holy crap, marriage, scratch that one, I don't want to know, la-la-la, not listening);
- Chocolate preference (milk, dark, or syrup);
- How often I'm supposed to call you (does texting count?);
- Favorite Starbucks drink (so I don't get dirty looks from or hit on by the barista again);
- Are you seeking a solution or do you just want to vent?

Now, wouldn't that be easier? Look at the time it would save. If there are certain instructions I can't follow, I'll kindly return the manual and dive back into the estrogen pool.

My manual is simple. Just keep your fingers out of my belly button. No, you're not allowed to ask why. I am *not* a freak. Maybe a weird uncle violated me. Find something else to diddle. Oh, and keep your damn tongue out of my ear. Who likes that anyway? I'm getting heebie-jeebies just typing this.

Some of the embarrassment an instruction manual would save includes:

- "Oh my God, he totally tried to... "
- "She has hairy nipples: hairier than mine. How does that happen?"
- "He sleeps with his dog. In fact, he spoons with his dog. God help me."
- "I was brushing my teeth, and she came in and sat on the pot right next to me ... mid-floss."
- "He has more porn than novels, and I found a Costco-sized tube of Astroglide in his pantry."
- "She licked the roof of my mouth and at one point I think our molars touched. How is that possible?"
- "I caught him shaving his taint ... with my razor."

Consider all the alcohol and cell minutes saved by knowing which buttons to push. Start assembling your manual today. I suggest a spiral binding and lamination. I have my highlighter and tool ready.

The Gatekeeper

I had an interesting night out in a college town recently with the good fortune of being the only man in a group of lovely girls their late twenties. The club caters to drinkers with training wheels. I felt like a proud father cheering from the sidelines most of the night. I ordered Scotch instead of flavored vodka, which got me sideways glances.

Prowling boys take an interesting path to the women around me. They see that I'm in the way of their prey. They size me up and wonder if I'm *with* one of the girls and if so, why. I can see their pickled brains working the angles. If I'm a sugar daddy, they can compete on a purely physical level for one night. If I'm not a sugar daddy, then they see a huge opening because the girl with me must have low self-esteem to be with such an "old man."

One of the puppies came up and started a conversation with me, the gatekeeper to the meat locker. He was twenty-four and we bonded on our East Coast origins. His strategy took an ugly turn when he discussed a dilemma he has with his forty-six-year-old father's thirty-one-year-old wife (bravo, by the way).

> Puppy: "Dude, it's just kind of gnarly, you know? She's all like closer to my age than his and hot."
> Gatekeeper: "And she's coming on to you?"
> Puppy: "Well, no, but she might, but I wouldn't do anything, man, that's sick."
> Gatekeeper: "Is it?"
> Puppy: "I mean she's my stepmom and stuff. But dude, you should see how she parades around the house."
> Gatekeeper: "Well son, since I'm older than your father, my advice is to find a safer place farther from home to plant your seed. Then you won't be cut off from your gravy train, take a deserved ass whooping from your father, and be sent packing back to where it snows a lot. Appearing on *Jerry Springer* shouldn't be a career goal, my child."

He laughed uncomfortably, tucked his tail between his legs, and scurried away. He started the avalanche, however. The boys kept a-coming, and they came through me. One actually wanted to hug me, to which I said, "Save the grind for the girls, Richard Simmons, we fist-tap here in sunny Man Diego."

How Single Are You?

I've recently noticed a certain kind of fellow bar patron who is hard to read. The loud and flamboyant people are hard to miss and easy to read. They flap around like birds doing mating calls. They wear loud "look-at-me" clothing: bright colors, tight or low-cut tops, and jeans with pocket glitz. They laugh louder than the average hyena. They hang in packs and tend to high-five, fist-tap, and hug excessively.

"Look-at-me" men have comments for every girl who passes by. Here are some memorable ones from a recent outing:

- "Nice shirt!"—It was what was *under* the shirt he was referring to.
- "Are you having fun?"—No, I have to pee.
- "Damn, girl" accompanied by a full body scan. I'm not sure where that one is heading, but I say dial 9-1 and keep your thumb on the 1.
- "How *you* doin'?"—I'm getting damp at the thought.

Girls seem to handle it so much better. They'll just smile, bat an eye, arch their back a little, or give that deadly over-the-shoulder glance. At that point, an unsolicited "hi" is usually about all they need to invest to get us slobbering.

Yet, there is the other kind of player: the disturbingly quiet and hard-to-read type. There are so many possible reasons why a person is quiet. They could be shy, calculating, stoned, or mute. They could be listening, daydreaming, married, or bored. I believe my shyness (in person, not in print) often makes me unapproachable because people have no idea how to take me. Am I a mass-murderer? A cop? A pervert? No, I'm a silent observer—as capable as the life-of-the-party man, minus the threat of puking on your carpet.

Men look at women the same way. Is she shy, uninterested, or two tequila shots from a freak? Is she waiting for her possessive boyfriend, hormonal, quietly sizing up her options, or just a cool mellow chick? She's going to be more work than Miss Look-at-my-Boobs, but she also could be well worth the effort. It's all so confusing.

Here's a solution: everyone's cell phone transmits his or her availability within a 100-foot radius. Call it GPS—Gross Percentage Single:

- 0% — Married earlier today and I'm pregnant.
- 10%—Married in the past year, no kids yet.
- 20%—Engaged and invitations have been sent.
- 30%—Married and husband is at a nudie bar.
- 40%—Married and husband is away on business, again.
- 50%—Dating the same man for less than three months.
- 60%—Married and husband forgot where my G-spot is.
- 70%—Dating the same man more than three months and he's not the same person he was during the first three months.
- 80%—Single but I hooked up last night.
- 90%—Single but I keep the ex's number handy.
- 100%—Single because I caught my man cheating on me last night with my best friend in my bed.

Think Ink

I'm not into tattoos, but it's certainly a huge market, especially in California. There are inked-up women, sleeved men, and the ultra-disturbing stretched ear lobe freaks all around. The tattoos on girls' lower backs have been nicknamed "tramp stamps." I assume that's because those girls are more sexually liberal.

As this is some prime real estate—sometimes more, sometimes less—I believe we need to consider other uses. We need to develop a lower back stamp that is erasable and begin to use that space for marketing, similar to "Golden Palace" ink on the backs of professional boxers.

As a marketing specialist, here are some of my suggestions for modernizing the tramp stamp into think ink:

- "Rest iPod here."
- "Slot B"
- Handlebars, Bull's-eye, or the Pacific Ocean—leaving Hawaii to be added by the viewer.
- "Second hole from the top, please."
- "Exit only."
- "Slippery when wet."
- "Yes we can, yes we are, and yes you will pay."
- "My name is _____ (in case you forgot)."
- "Don't mess my hair."
- "Generic Viagra — $1.25"
- 1-800-ENLARGE
- "My brother is a cop."
- "Ring size seven, square-cut, antique platinum setting, two-carat minimum."
- "Stop watching TV and concentrate."

Corporate Holiday Parties Suck

Here are the top ten holiday party gifts:

1. The girlfriend or wife gets to see and often meet the little flowers decorating her man's office. They're all so ripe and tempting to pollinate.

Men think that we are disarming the situation by introducing our work "associate" to our girl. We say, "Honey, this is the Amy that I work with on the Acme project." Our girl hears, "Honey, if I haven't dipped my pen in this company ink yet it isn't for lack of trying." Women can sense our nonsense.
2. Alcohol shows a whole other side of us best left to the imagination. We've all seen the dance floor charades (mating calls) of the short-skirted after too many Cosmos.
3. Work talk is boring the daylights out of our dates. Is it any wonder they are glassy-eyed and becoming best friends with the bartender? Pass the bar nuts.
4. Learning the personal life of people you really don't care to know outside of work. Finding out that your associate enjoys skeet shooting, line dancing, and nude sunbathing doesn't make working with him any easier.
5. Approaching (or being approached by) the boss doesn't provide many opportunities for career advancement. I had a boss attempt to chest-bump me, like pro football players do after a touchdown. It ended up being his chest, my face, and my sprint to the bar for a double Scotch on the rocks.
6. Gossip flourishes. All the office girls get out the cat claws and file them into fashion-and-personality slicing and dicing weapons of mass destruction. "Can you believe she is wearing that prom dress? Are those Kmart shoes? Where did she buy those boobs? Her hair looks like straw; dye much,

honey? She's totally doing Keith in Finance while her husband has the kids at soccer practice."
7. The entertainment wouldn't have been entertaining even twenty years ago, when the music they're playing was actually popular. There's a good reason why "Celebration," "Mony, Mony," "Old Time Rock & Roll," and "The Electric Slide" are no longer on the radio. I hear them at a company function and the bile starts rising.
8. If you have subordinates at the function, they study everything you do. They will order a drink when you do, of similar strength. They will kiss up—including to your spouse—because it's bonus time. They will be on their best behavior until you turn your back.
9. Guys feel a strange need to increase their displays of masculinity by breaking out the cigars, doing shots, and high-fiving for no apparent reason. Watch Mr. VP down three Jägerbombs then stagger around the dance floor with his shirt half untucked, tie stained, and hairpiece askew.
10. Monday's long hours avoiding eye contact.

Be Nice and Lie to Me

What's worse than having your feelings hurt? The mental pain usually comes with physical pain as well. We're distracted, can't stop thinking about it, and often lose sleep over it. We think of ways we could have responded to defend our pride. We consider retaliation. We become sad and feel unwanted or picked on. Since we all have experienced this pain, we're nice to people and often tell them what they want to hear, not what we mean.

I don't see anything wrong with a white lie, to tell you the truth (pun intended). There are different severities, and I do endorse the covert angles over the patronizing ones. For example, if your woman says, "How do you like my outfit?" and the truth is you hate it, you can say:

- "Wow honey, you look awesome! I love it."
- "Very nice, dear."
- "You know, it's lovely *but* that little black dress you have just *makes me melt*."
- "Whatever you feel most comfortable in."
- "Um, not so much."
- "No, Cyndi Lauper, I can't allow you to leave the house in that."

More patronizing answers are at the top and more truthful at the bottom. I have found the safest place is somewhere in the middle. It also depends on the importance of the question, right? If it's something I honestly don't have an opinion about, then it isn't as important to be honest. Although not having an opinion isn't the same as not caring, it can still get me into hot water.

The key is to know your audience. Women are often looking for confirmation, not the truth. Men don't ask enough and more often *need* the truth.

What about something touchy like, "How do you feel about me?" That's a tough one because what they're really asking is, "Do you feel about me as strongly as I feel about you?" It's tricky because you don't really know how strongly the other one feels. Worse yet, you can't go by what they told you recently because they may have told *you* what *you* needed to hear. It is so confusing. Even a hesitation in answering is dangerous. How about, "I like you a little bit more than you like me," as a safe response?

Add in the fact that, consciously or not, we're manipulating our mates into the position we desire. I'm OK with someone telling me what I need to hear. Sometimes I allow myself to be manipulated. If it makes a person happy then why shouldn't I? Let's continue lying to be kind.

Uninvited

Let's see where we all draw the line on this one. If you got laid this morning, it probably will be a more solid line. There are different levels of commitment in relationships. Even marriage itself has unique commitment interpretations. The near unanimous boundary is around sex. If you're in a committed relationship you're not allowed to have sex (even oral, Mr. President) with another person. Even that gets fuzzy. I bet that most husbands could forgive the wife who "kissed a girl."

Let's break it down to two angles:

1. You're tempted by a person in a committed relationship.
2. You're in a committed relationship and tempted by another person.

By "tempted," I mean you desire to share some physical affection with them, not just look at them, point, and say, "Pretty! Me likey." I've been in both situations, so I think I can relate.

What about the case of the single man and the committed woman? At first glance, men can easily assess the attraction. Before she looks our way, we can tell if it is physically possible. From that point, if there is flirtation that attraction can grow. If we see a ring, that can be a good thing (*gasp*) or a bad thing. If the potential is purely physical—with no mental connection at all—then it can be a good thing if she is committed because we have short-term goals in mind anyway. We hope that she does too or it can get ugly.

If, on the other hand, the attraction is more than physical, then further analysis (and alcohol) is required. If the man is mentally stimulated—it can happen—but for the committed woman the attraction is purely physical, she becomes a challenge. We're so damn competitive. Even when lesser opponents abound, we are attracted to the game we can't win, because we're the underdog.

When you play this game out, if the man can pry her away, he usually loses interest right after success. How cruel and unfortunate. If he is stiff-armed, then the woman can preserve her commitment and enjoy her secret fantasy while leaving him to drown his sorrows.

What about the case of the married man and the temptress? People say, "If you are having your needs met at home you won't wander." I'm sorry, but that's bullshit. The reason is *nobody* has *all* of their needs met in one place *all* of the time. I have seen men in nearly perfect relationships tempted by women who don't offer one-tenth of what they have at home. There are nagging thoughts like "Who will know?" and "What am I missing?" If the men don't follow through it's usually because they have had enough time to assess the potential future damage. Yet, it's amazing how we can postpone that internal discussion.

Like the rest of life, it's subjective and complicated. I can write novels on my experiences alone. I love thinking about the taboo and questioning why things are taboo and to what degree. Where do we draw the line? Are you cheating the minute you think about relations with a committed person? When you flirt? When you share intimate thoughts? When you discuss your spouse's inadequacies with someone else? When you dance? When you kiss? When you touch? When you sleep together?

Where is your line and does your partner know?

Black Specks in the Diamond

Diamonds are incredibly beautiful, but if you look closely, you'll find flaws. It's how jewelers find a fake. Fakes won't have flaws. This applies to the people in your life as well. We all have flaws and, in fact, since the word "flaw" is subjective we may or may not be aware of them. If you're in a trusting relationship, and you feel the need to look for evidence to the contrary, you'll probably find it—unless they're faking it.

Let me illustrate with a recent phenomenon that has come about with the advent of text messaging. Have you ever gone through your mate's cell phone? Have you been tempted? If you went through it, I bet you found something that unnerved you. It may have been completely harmless but in our drama-filled world, it just takes a little imagination to spin the insignificant event into a bad day.

My solution: lock your damn cell phone! You're not going to remove the desire and curiosity your mate has to dig for dirt, but you can make it difficult. Many will take this "locking of the phone" as an act of guilt concealment. I disagree. I call it privacy. When I go into the bathroom, I close the door behind me. If you sneak in you're going to find something unattractive, so why do it?

I know of someone recently booted by his fiancée because she found an incriminating message on his phone. I don't know these people well enough to be confident that anything took place to justify her violent reaction (which included a Blackberry smashing … *horrors*). She found a message from his ex that said something to the effect, "Let me know the next time you're in town, and I'll give you a welcome back BJ … ha ha ha." Definitely cringe-worthy, but is it a showstopper?

I know that if an ex sent me a message like that she would definitely be kidding, not just because of the "ha ha ha," but because I'm the generous type preferring to give than receive. (OK, now I *am* kidding, but you might have just cringed.) Oh come on, women don't send messages like that with literal intent, do they? Maybe I'm deluded or maybe I need to stop dating good girls. Seriously, it was a flirtatious note, but I'm going to have to side with the defendant, not just because we share genders.

It takes less than one minute to lock your phone, so do it. If your mate raises an eyebrow, simply say, "I'm sorry, honey, but I prefer privacy and since I also respect yours, you should lock your phone as well." While you're at it, change your password on your email away from your pet's name and any combination of your birth date. If you don't, somebody might see your black specks, my diamond.

The Perfect Kiss

Almost fifty years on earth and I still haven't figured this one out. No, I'm not confessing to being a poor kisser. I can't predict how my woman wants to be kissed. Then, once we kiss, I'm not sure if they are kissing me the way they think I want to be kissed or the way *they* want to be kissed. Maybe this all belongs in the instruction manual: "How Do I Work You?"

There are extremes, including the stiff-lipped peck and the face-swallowing, molar-touching slop fest. I reserve the stiff-lipped peck for the aunt, co-worker, or friend's wife with whom you want to clearly convey that it was borderline inappropriate and most usually unwanted. It is best to dry your lips on your sleeve before the kiss, to avoid wrong impressions.

The other extreme (ole face-suck) can be equally as gross as kissing your aunt. Some women, in my experience, really do enjoy esophagus exploration. One I dated enjoyed it so much so that I had to fight to stop from laughing. I think I tore the corners of my lips trying to open as wide and at one point, the tip of my nose got wet. When I slid away to her neck she monkey-dicked my ear so bad that I felt like I had just gone down a water-slide.

Kissing is essential in a good relationship, a showstopper if it's horrible. How do you convey to the other—without hurting their feelings—that too much or too little slop is going on? Do you bite their tongue? No, that doesn't work, as I'm sure there are people that either like that or will return your bite thinking you do. Ugh.

I guess we could talk to our kisser about it, right? We could say something gentle, like, "You know, I have really sensitive lips, and I enjoy touching them lightly with your wonderful soft lips. Occasionally we can add the gentle touching of the tips of our tongues: brief enough that we never experience that embarrassing spit tightrope when we pull away." How would that work? Oh, some people would be offended because we all think we're a lot better at everything (including kissing and driving) than we really are.

In any successful relationship, communication is the key. It's a matter of deciding if the words need to be spoken. Hopefully, body language is sufficient without an increased chance of misinterpretation. We wouldn't want to cause more of the pain we're trying to avoid. Why does it all have to be so complicated?

Random Things about Me

My chest hair was once used to string a Stradivarius.

I was contracted to knock down the Berlin Wall, with my penis.

I was abducted by aliens who paid (and tipped) me to probe them.

After three bean enchiladas, I once farted the national anthem at Petco Park.

I made Madonna blush.

Kurt Warner thanked me instead of Jesus.

When I was an altar boy, a Catholic priest wined and dined me before molesting me.

I was once sued by a predominantly female corporation for *not* harassing them.

The Panama Canal? Been there, dug that.

My bladder is so big that I started the Venice floods.

I hit a baseball so far that they named a moon crater after me.

I killed Jack Bauer, with my bare hands.

My ex offered to pay me sperm support.

Obama took dance lessons from me.

J-Lo offered to change her name to J-To.

The Chief of Police served me chilled shots of Patron Tequila at a DUI checkpoint.

While surfing, I was safely guided to shore by a great white shark.

My sweat has been used to remove crow's-feet wrinkle lines.

Paris Hilton left my hotel room smiling and limping.

My cats are so brilliant they finish my crossword puzzles, in the dark.

Women drop Rufis in their own drinks when they see me coming.

I threw a baseball so fast that it created a black hole.

Trojan uses me as a model for their molds, pre-erection.

Simon Cowell asked me to sing at his wedding.

I convinced people how silly it is to write "Random Things" because nobody really cares.

Carlsbad Cougar Runs from Atheist

An interesting thing happened at a local wine bar. A group of girls (all coincidentally thirty-nine) came in and bellied up next to me. I remained open-minded to the possibility that one or more (OK, more likely fewer) of these women could represent an opportunity to spread my genes. Did I finally find a host for my evil seed?

One smiled flirtatiously and asked what I was drinking. I confessed that I'm no wine expert, and I humbly take what the experts (bartenders) recommend. I offered her a taste. She accepted. I'm in, right? Not yet.

The flirtation was kicked up a notch. I'm a veteran, so sure, I played along. I had just seen a video about the discrimination a poor high school student went through, so I thought I'd try an experiment. Surely, a liberal Left Coaster in heat wouldn't be frightened by my lack of faith in the supernatural. Or would she?

We continued flirting away with the usual comments. "What do you do?" "Do you have kids?" "You have pretty eyes." Then there was the gentle touching of my hand. Then she performed the caretaker test by squeezing my upper arm. Her girlfriends were also sizing me up to see if they would let her continue or toss her under a bus, the way only male friends do best.

She admitted that she was in the middle of a nasty divorce. That can be good, short term. She also had children ... OK, shorter term. Sorry, that was rude of me, but I just *thought* it, I didn't say it. Then the girls all sat at a table and invited me over, which started the cross-examination.

"So Phil, why are you single?"

"I'm a tough match," I replied.

"No, come on, you're cute. How are you a tough match?"

"Well, I'm the 'a' word. No, not 'alcoholic' ... 'atheist.'"

"What? You mean you don't believe in anything?"

"No, that's not what it means. It means I don't believe in supernatural beings."

"Well, you need to have your Chakras cleared. Have you done that?"

"Umm…"

"I'm addicted to acupuncture," her friend jumped in.

"God is like … an 'energy,' you know?" another quipped.

"Really," I responded, seeing this was not going to go well.

"Oh, you mean you're spiritual, not religious, right?"

Now, my genetic syringe had a different response than my brain did. It was a legendary struggle, but the wine yet again removed my filter, and I said, "No, I'm not spiritual and I don't have any Chakras, but I have been known to clear a chocolate mousse."

That pretty much sealed the deal. I was definitely going home empty-handed. They recoiled from me quicker than if I had confessed to having the flu, genital warts, and an obsession with feeding pugs to coyotes.

I guess it's back to the drawing board for this infidel.

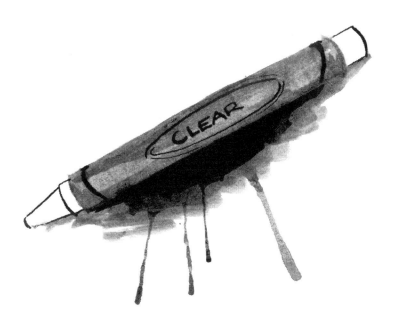

Tag, I'm It

Were you named after anyone? Three kings, two fathers, and an uncle.

When was the last time you cried? When I pulled a nose hair.

Do you like your handwriting? What's handwriting? WTF? LOL.

What is your favorite lunchmeat? Tofurkey and blood pudding.

Do you have kids? Yes, millions of them waiting to infect the world.

If you were another person, would you be friends with you? If I had good taste, yes.

Do you use sarcasm? Who, me?

Do you still have your tonsils? Yes, I pick up sushi rolls with them.

Would you bungee jump? No, but I would point and laugh if someone died trying.

What is your favorite cereal? Dark chocolate-covered raisins in vanilla soymilk.

Do you untie your shoes when you take them off? I only wear loafers, flip-flops, and fuck-me pumps.

What is your favorite position? Pitcher.

What is your favorite ice cream? Filet mignon.

What is the first thing you notice about people? Acne or a cleft palate.

What is your least favorite thing about yourself? That I waste time answering stupid questions.

Who do you miss the most? Curly Howard.

What color pants and shoes are you wearing? I can't tell. They're around my ankles.

What are you listening to right now? Clicking keys.

If you were a crayon, what color would you be? Clear.

Who was the last person you talked to on the phone? Joe from Customer Service in India.

Favorite sports to watch? Porn.

Hair color? No.

Eye color? White with some red (if I'm stoned) and blue.

Do you wear contacts? Sorry, I can't see this question.

Favorite food? Cake batter.

Scary movies or happy endings? After a massage? Do I really have to answer this?

Summer or Winter? Both are talented, but Summer gives a better lap dance.

Favorite dessert? Sleep.

What is on your mouse pad? Blood.

What did you watch on TV last night? Tiny colored pixels.

Favorite sound(s)? Metallica('s).

Rolling Stones or Beatles? Throwing stones at beetles.

Do you have a special talent? Yes, I can predict the past.

Where were you born? Mars, or so I'm told.

How did you meet your spouse/significant other? I drugged her.

She Said She Was Happy, Very Sadly

Sit with an empty chair next to you in a San Diego wine bar and it's like opening a book. It's an ideal place to open a therapy practice. They even have couches. I could call it "Brain Massages by Phil."

A recent "patient" was an attractive nature girl in her thirties, newly engaged to a Brazilian. He was away at the Lakers game, so she donned the clingy low-cut dress and furry-top jacket and sought wine and conversation. That's brave for a young woman, but I admire it and hope the trend continues.

She spent most of the two hours trying to convince me how happy she was. Or, perhaps she was trying to convince herself. As the words came out her body language and expression didn't match. It was uncomfortable. I realized I was not a romantic option for her so I wasn't pursuing that angle. We were just talking.

They dated for three years and were now living together. She explained that she was supporting him until recently as he was working to get certification. Now he is working and self-sufficient. I asked why she wasn't at the Lakers game with him, and she said it was a "work thing." The game was on the TV at the bar and was exciting, so I assured her that he would enjoy it even with his typical South American soccer obsession.

After the game ended, she called him to see how he enjoyed it. Her expression changed quickly and she hung up. I asked what that was about, and she said he told her he was driving in traffic and couldn't talk. She figured he would spend the night in L.A. at a friend's house. I could tell she was sad and hurt, but she faked a smile.

I wanted to shake her. "Demand better for yourself. You're about to marry this man, have his children, and tie yourself to him for twenty years. Is this all you expect? You're here all sexy and sad, and he's in play land. He doesn't have enough time or respect for you to pull over and talk? He is taking you for granted. At least tell him you won't stand for it." Naturally, I said nothing of the sort, just the generic: "I see."

She stewed for a few more minutes, put her chin in her hand, sipped some wine, and then said, "I need a cigarette." I know I have a big "rescue complex" where for some strange reason I feel it's my responsibility to care, defend, and protect. It must be biologically encoded. Imagine that: I have morality without faith. It was none of my business, so I paid my tab, gave her a hug, and walked away.

It's sad to see such beauty covered in sadness. Sure, doctors will prescribe something to obscure the sadness obscuring the beauty. But drugs only add layers, drive the sickness deeper, and make it more difficult to heal. I can't help her. Maybe I did by just listening and not judging (verbally). I hope to see her again—with fewer clouds next time.

Trying on Shoes

That's my dating life. I apologize in advance. This essay is filled with self-deprecation and is not an indictment of anyone I have dated (or will soon date) who happens to have done the precarious thing of buying this book. There are numerous comfortable, classy, and attractive shoes that

I'll never own. Similarly, there are many women that don't fit. So, this shouldn't be offensive. Oh, how I hate feigning political correctness. Go ahead, laugh, or be offended. I'm just here to get a reaction anyway.

So, how is my dating life like trying on shoes? Well, I seem to have no problem finding awesome shoes and I'm fortunate enough to afford most of them. I can't seem to find any that fit. I know, I know ... I should wear them for a while and break them in. Well, what if I invest all that time and end up with bunions? It's best to try on a variety of shoes, take home ones that fit, and give them away when they cause discomfort.

Here are some interesting parallels between my shoes and my women:

- I admire them even when I can't have them.
- I'm overconfident that they'd look better on me.
- Some are best at certain events only.
- My friends love to criticize mine, but they're just jealous and have awful taste.
- I don't let my mother pick them out for me.
- Sometimes older ones are softer, more comfortable, and easier to slip in and out of.
- Flashy, loud ones are usually more expensive and wear out more quickly.
- Ones I find online rarely arrive as advertised.
- Athletic ones seem to get dirty more quickly.
- Some look incredible but become dull and painful after a few hours.
- Some are too narrow or too wide.
- I have had my toes curled by a few.

I've been advised to just pick some and take the time to get used to them. But I'm an impatient shopper. I would rather take three home, and return the ones that don't fit right. I do try to return them in original condition but sometimes I leave a scuff or two with my caustic opinions and beliefs. Damaged goods are still *goods*, right?

Maybe I'm destined to try on dozens because I'm a tough fit. It certainly will be a stretch; lots of flexibility will be required to spend significant time with me. Until I find the right pair, I guess I'll have to toughen up and get used to the occasional pain caused by going without.

Three Things

Three names I go by:

1. Dude
2. Man
3. Such an asshole

SUCH A NICE GUY

Three jobs I have had in my life:

1. Buy women wine
2. Buy women dinner
3. Buy women taxi rides home

Three places I have lived:

1. A barstool
2. La-Z-Boy
3. In line at Starbucks

Three TV shows that I watch:

1. Fox 5 Weather with Chrissy Russo
2. Chrissy Russo on Fox 5 Weather
3. Chelsea Lately

Three places I have been:

1. In bed
2. Hovering over the toilet
3. In the shower

Three people who email me regularly:

1. V1@gra
2. C1@lis
3. En1@arge

Three of my favorite foods:

1. Thigh sweat
2. Earlobe dew
3. Neck mist

Three of my favorite stores:

1. Hustler
2. Any wine store
3. Medicinal marijuana outlets

Three things I am looking forward to:

1. Churches closing
2. Finding lace thongs in my sheets
3. Sleeping in

Three friends I think might react to this:

1. Jesus (not the messiah, my gardener)
2. A couple of exes
3. Chrissy Russo's attorney

The Committed Should Be Committed

Depending on where you put the emphasis in that title, it certainly can be interpreted differently. I'm intending the second "committed" to refer to the act of sending someone to a mental institution for treatment.

I met two women recently (yes, at the local watering hole) who were out for their quarterly night away from the husbands and children. They seemed to relish their rare night out. It's interesting how women polish up with their nicest clothes and accessories for these outings. Isn't it funny how men do nothing of the sort when we get a fun pass?

One woman mentioned that she had been married for ten years. I congratulated her but why did I do that? It was reflexive. Why does she deserve congratulations? I don't know if she is happy. Well, she seemed happy so let's assume she truly is happily married. If I had told her I was wearing the same shirt that I have worn for ten years (happily, even), would she have congratulated me? What if I was driving the same car? Was in the same job? Only visiting that particular restaurant? Using the same sheets (because they're comfortable)?

My point is that maybe, just maybe, extended commitment is no longer something we should envy or congratulate. Sure, it had practical application back in humanity's youth. A dedicated partner provides strength in numbers and the sharing of duties. Is a good partnership good enough or the best it could be? Aren't we taking a large gamble for a small amount of social admiration? Face it, when we commit, we are settling for what odds say is probably not the ideal long-term situation. Mr. Right-now is probably not Mr. Right-next-to-you-on-your-death-bed as in *The Notebook*.

I don't mean to be a big downer on relationships. Society puts too much pressure on us to make it last. In fact, if you change partners too often that implies some deficiency, perversion, or immaturity. That's nonsense.

Isn't it more pathological to stay in unhealthy long-term relationships that have run their course than leaving before the mold appears?

Do you find the beginning of a relationship more or less exciting than the middle? Do you find the prospect of a new lover exciting, even when it's taboo? Of course you do. Some people say that's why we fantasize. I say that is what choice is all about. If you sit at the same blackjack table long enough, you're going to lose. No matter how much in love you are, when a better option comes along you are taking a risk by not taking *the* risk.

People are afraid of moving on, not only because of social pressure. There's also the fear that your next lover will be hard to find and could turn out to be worse than your current lover. Well, to my point, if extended commitment is not the goal, you can quickly, easily, and guiltlessly leave any relationship, and *you should*.

We should concentrate on draining every drop from a relationship while it's ripe, so there are no regrets. Once the passion is gone and better options abound, move on. You'll be doing your partner a favor while keeping your selfish genes satisfied.

Hot for Teacher

Did you ever have a crush on a teacher? I sure did. I remember Ms. M. back in high school. She was sexy, smart, and would do those little things (and it doesn't take much) to drive the high school boys crazy. She had this bad (in a good way) habit of sitting on the corner of my desk during a lecture. She wore tight sweaters and floral perfume, which often made my trip to the next class uncomfortable.

She caught me telling a friend how she was making me crazy. She said that I shouldn't talk behind people's backs, with a smirk. I just stuttered, stammered, and said "but I'm in front of you." It was witty, but fruitless.

I'm sure it's different for girls but when we boys hit about thirteen, we enter the confusing struggle of mind versus genitals. It didn't take much at all. I could be flipping through the JC Penney catalog while on the throne, and if I happened upon the bra section, I'd find myself wedged under the toilet seat.

I shouldn't be embarrassed about it because it's natural. Obviously, some biological trigger happens once mating is possible. Yet, we hide sex from teens because they're not mature enough to handle themselves responsibly. That's probably true in some cases, but I think it would be better to inform them than forbid them. Forbidding them only increases their curiosity and desire.

Let's say, for instance, that Ms. M. found something sexy about my seventeen-year-old 132-pound pasty frame featuring five chest hairs and acne. Oh, it can happen. (But no, it didn't.) Then, after three martinis she drops her inhibitions and decides to make an indelible impression on the student body. There's something to be said for having a willing and eager trainee. So, we get a little crazy and do the forbidden deed.

I'd be receiving all kinds of accolades from my friends, and she'd be receiving a nasty career-ending prison sentence. There was nothing forced or unwanted. However, if I was four months from my eighteenth birthday and she was twenty-four, it wouldn't matter. I know I was immature, but I wouldn't be able to bring myself to the conclusion that I was taken advantage of. There would be no emotional scars and one sweet memory to recall as needed.

Now, switch genders and we have an even more serious problem. Forget the fact that girls mature much more quickly. If some male teacher hooks up with a female student, he's in big trouble. Biologically speaking, she is a more suitable mate than women are in their forties yet this is a major taboo. I'm not condoning it but I wonder if this is such a serious crime if it's consensual.

Well, Ms. M. remains a fantasy of thirty years ago, so even though nothing ever happened I can rearrange my wine-soaked brain cells to have a compelling story for the bocce club someday.

What Are You On?

I can identify any intentionally induced affliction people have, without a blood test. Alcohol and marijuana are easy to detect. Coke and ecstasy are a little more difficult but still obvious. But there is a new affliction that is legal and confounds the shit out of me: antidepressants.

I don't recall ever being clinically depressed, so I'm fortunate. I have definitely been sad when dealing with the death of a relative, nursing homes, and a divorce. I don't think it was ever to the point where I could get a prescriptive cure. Then again, maybe all it takes nowadays is seeing a doctor and asking for drugs.

Whatever the case may be, I can tell when someone is off-kilter and recreational drugs are not the cause. I'm beginning to suspect antidepressants are the culprit. Drunks are easy to detect. There is mild retardation of the motor skills (or gravy-leg, as I like to call it) and speech slurring. Stoners have the telltale dime-slit eyes, sheepish grin, and inappropriate laughter followed by paranoia.

How do I identify somebody looped on Prozac? Here are some of the signs confirmed by a mess of a woman I met recently:

- The person's eyes seem to split and see around my head although they are looking directly at me. She catches me turning around to see if there is an angry ex heading my way, which only adds to the confusion.
- Comical constant repetition: "Where are you from? Are you from around here? I live in San Diego, I mean I can't give you my address, yet, but I live near here. Do you … live … like, around here?" At this point, I'm tempted to don the Hindu accent and say I live in Jakarta.
- Delayed reactions to my jokes or teasing. This is uncomfortable because I try not to laugh at my own jokes but then I get the blank stare as they try to be pissed at me while the Xanax blocks the anger.

- She mistakes my sarcasm for honesty. How many times must I hear "Really?" when I speak of my huge black penis, which fathered the Octomom's litter?

I need more training in the mood-altering medication field. Maybe the answer is to experiment with some myself. I could load up on Zoloft and attend a Bible study, seeing how long it takes people to notice the "666" tattooed on my knuckles. I could simply wander around Costco with an empty child's seat cart asking people if they found my Mexican midget lover. I don't mean *midget-lover*, that would be gross. I mean lover who happens to be a midget. Better yet, I could attend a line-dancing competition in rollerblades and assless chaps.

Grumpy Old Man

We are fortunate to have a coastal train that runs from North County to the Padres games. Convenience comes with a price and I'm not referring to the paltry $12 roundtrip ticket; that's a bargain. After taking four trips during the first week of the baseball season, here is my list of advantages and disadvantages:

Advantage: Saturday's car was loaded with a dozen girls in their twenties on their way to a bachelorette party. They were giddy, in their tiny black dresses, and drinking Cosmopolitans from penis straws. It was so cute that I almost cried. It was like watching kittens play: too cute to put into words. This helps me understand why terrorists strap bombs to themselves. No, not for the twenty virgins—to stop the screeching voices.
Disadvantage: Being old without evidence of wealth, a magnum of Grey Goose, and a bag of weed. I was sadly unprepared.

Advantage: I brought two perfectly chilled Hefeweizens along for the ride.
Disadvantage: A group of twenty-one-year-old (yeah right) dudes half-cocked on Milwaukee's Best repeating the same story for sixty minutes about how they got into a street fight. The words "like," "totally," "gnarly," "dude," "amped," and other gems were repeated often enough for me to consider jumping out of the lead car onto the tracks in front of the train.

Advantage: I have my new best friend, Kindle (no, that isn't a goddamn dog, Google it, for Christ's sake), with me to keep me company and grant me solitude.
Disadvantage: "Dude, what's that? Is that like one of those new Amazon things? Do you like it? My cousin has one. How does it work? Can you get the newspaper on it?

It's expensive, huh. I'm going to wait until it comes down in price. What are you reading?"

I think I have officially turned into that grumpy old neighbor we all had. You know, the geezer in the robe who would yell and shake his paper at us if we stepped on his lawn. Is this what I have to look forward to? I have hair where I don't want it instead of where I need it and an insatiable urge to slap youngsters about the head with a *Wall Street Journal*. Zeus, save me!

The Cougar

I watched TVLand's *The Cougar* about a forty-year-old real estate specialist sifting through twenty boys—yes, I said *boys*, not *men*—to pick the child that could be her future husband. This has train-wreck written all over it, and

I'm not one to turn away from the carnage. Allow me to get a little catty and do a some crime scene investigation.

First of all, Stacy, "cougar" is a derogatory term no matter how often you call yourself "the cougar." If I *say* I'm an asshole, saying it doesn't make me any less of an asshole, just an observant asshole.

Vivica Fox (her "A" is certainly not missing or silent: it's wonderful and trailing close behind her) asks her if the men are "young enough." These hairless puppies range from twenty-three to twenty-seven, and she's forty so what could be younger? Do we need to recruit from Little League practice? Stacy likes the young ones because they are "not intimidated" by her success. No kidding, Ms. Shallow, they aren't attracted to it either. They couldn't care less if you work at Denny's or own Denny's. What matters is if you can drop to your knees as quickly as Yankee catcher Jorge Posada.

Being a cougar means you are not "in your prime," as you stated, it means you are way past it, trying to cling and compete by using an arsenal of Botox, hair dye, and liposuction. It also means you are simply a condom-less option and an easy one at that.

"Stacy's like a gray squirrel I just want to pounce on," one faux-hawked infant professed. I don't get the metaphor. Is the gray thing referring to her nether region where the coloring doesn't take as well? Who wants to pounce on a squirrel? Isn't she more like a frizzy, worn-out, fish-scented (ouch) toy that cats want to pounce on?

Stacy says just because she likes younger men doesn't mean she likes immature men. Oh, so they have to be potty-trained and wash their hands after peeing. Those are awful high barriers to entry there, missy. You're one selective señorita.

"If men can do it, so can women." Do what? Date younger women? Well, sure women can do it, but TVLand is missing an essential element. *Ugly and fat* older men can do it. Does that work for women? Umm, nope. Find me twenty youngsters who would emasculate themselves for a shot at Betty White, Joan Rivers, or Kathy Bates.

"When I told you that you have my heart, I meant it," confesses one of the lapdogs. He meant that she had one of his Nintendo controllers stuck up her beaver and her extensions were blocking his view. That's a big deal because she was biting into his recess time.

"I'm ready to make that physical connection … that she wants," says another crooner. Here, young grasshopper, is the physical connection she wants: your stubbly chest and cattle prod for the thirty seconds it's going to take you to finish (which is about four minutes and thirty seconds less than her fame will last).

"I actually have a daughter that is older than you," confesses the cougar. Now, I'm going to call shenanigans here because the next clip shows the boys all distraught with that confession. I think they spliced their reaction to her confession about her herpes instead. Even these mental midgets would be nothing short of elated to know that Baby Mommy's Baby is legal tender and will no doubt be prancing around the den in a T-shirt and pink panties. Ah, there's nothing better than having backup booty around.

"A show that will change everything you know about relationships, love, and getting older." Oh, will it? Are you talkin' to me? Hey, I slept with a forty-plus cougar back in the '80s before they were cougars. I was a ripe twenty-five and welcomed the shot at the sauced financially secure older woman. She didn't require any upfront investment of dinner, flowers, and emotional pleadings. I know damn well what getting older means, TVLand. For me, it means I can still drink from the fountain of youth without a production crew, surgery, and point-and-laugh fame. All I need is a little—OK, and sometimes a lot of—alcohol, timing, and a sense of humor.

Home Field Advantage

This is not about me. It is not about any girl I have dated. It is hypothetical. I'm just curious, so I'm making up different scenarios to try to understand what women want.

Let's say this man and woman head into date number four. The previous dates began with flirting, dinner, some playful arm or thigh touching, and a hug and quick kiss goodnight. The second date progressed into a Cabernet-induced make-out session, which got the fellow some side boob touching and perhaps a lower hip, upper butt-cheek drive by. Then there was the pregame warm-up of date number three, which included a face-slopping couch straddle complete with hip grinding and through the shirt groping.

So here we (I mean *they*) are at date number four. The grounds crew had all the preparations in order. The sheets were clean (especially the pillowcases, as mascara stains can result in a technical foul and game misconduct). The guest toothbrush was placed in an inaccessible bin along with old condom wrappers and movie tickets. All porn was hidden. Any recently discovered stray earrings were removed from bedside tables.

In the personal hygiene area, the man has done some edging and trimming and even touched up the undercarriage with some deodorant not typically designed for said area. He also primed the pump to avoid an embarrassing misfire. However, he has still gone through the litany of excuses in case of emergency including my favorite: "You know, you are so hot that I just can't control myself. Give me fifteen minutes and you can put me back in, coach. Consider this my first charged timeout."

Now it's game on! (Insert your own gory details here.) Post-game scenarios are equally challenging. Once the final buzzer goes off, how soon before the teams separate and the equipment is removed from the playing field? If the equipment was protected, then this better happen quickly as to not accidentally leave the protection behind, which is embarrassing to find and remove. The snapping sound of slipped condom retrieval is also worthy of a flagrant foul.

In the case where no tarp was used, there is most likely some excess moisture (oh, I know, not a popular word with the fairer gender). The dilemma here is how to take care of the "wet spot," with one of the options being just allow it to evaporate, although that adds to laundry chores and detectable culpability. So, is the best option to head for the towels and if so, how long to wait before bounding to the bathroom? Should the man hand the towel to the woman or wipe her field-of-play for her?

Then we have the post-game interview. Is it best to line up the critics immediately and stare at the scorecards or just cuddle and talk about the weather? I guess that depends on how good you think your performance was. It really doesn't matter because you're not going to get the true critique. Her best friend is, on her ride home.

Subsequently, something uncomfortable comes up. I'll keep it clean and come up with an analogy. A baseball field is designed for baseball. So, why do dates eight through ten involve trying to play baseball on a soccer field, mall parking lot, sofa, bathtub, car, lawn, neighbor's bathroom, hotel room deck, and public hot tub or pool? What about safety and comfort? Misuse of playing fields may result in injury, performance anxiety, and public humiliation. Boy, good thing this isn't about me.

Net Mating Benefit

In Steve Harvey's book *Act Like a Lady, Think Like a Man*, he says that men instantly size up women they meet, trying to decide if they want to sleep with them and how much it will cost to do so. I call it a net mating benefit (NMB) calculation. Steve doesn't go into the actual calculations, so allow me, a math nerd, to attempt to assemble a formula for NMB.

Size matters. Of course it does. I have heard the claim from some of my swine brothers that big girls work harder. That makes this part of the formula a difficult calculation. If the woman is thin to the point where I can see veins and ribs, I know she's probably going to set those expectations on me. I'm not about to trade chocolate, wine, and pasta for broccoli, bottled water, and cob salads. I can't see myself in those goofy biker outfits or doing anything that ends in "thon." Then again, if she has a muffin-top and cellulite-laden arms, it will bring on performance anxiety.

Height matters. Tall girls are sexy but I can't handle it when their hands and feet are bigger than mine are. I guess because of similar male myths, I fear my luggage may be lost in the oversized bin. If I ever hear, "Is it in yet?" I will need years of therapy. I prefer a woman who will fit under my arm without dislocating my shoulder. When dancing, she can look up into my eyes, reach up to wrap her arms around my neck, and bury her head in my chest. If she is looking down at me and resting her arms on my shoulders, I feel like I'm dancing with my third grade teacher.

Gray matters. This can also go both ways. Smart girls are sexy, but they can be intimidating. I often feel like they are checking my grammar and looking for inconsistencies between my words and my actions. They tend to overanalyze everything from the things I say, work I do, books I read, and porn (I mean *TV*) I watch. They don't always say it to me, but I know they're taking mental notes that they'll share with their friends or mother. Ah, the raised eyebrow: it doesn't bode well. Dummies are often boring as hell to spend clothed time with but they can be entertaining.

NET MATING BENEFIT

A drunken dummy can provide priceless memories as long as she's gone before she stains the carpets.

Equipment matters. Boobs and butt are the two most distracting things in the world next to a bloody car crash and a marijuana crop. Show too much, though, and even a dimwit knows it's compensating for something bad. A tiny bit of lace showing above the jean line or the hint of a nipple will send us sideways. We're so damn immature that it takes all the restraint in the world to keep from jumping up and down, pointing, grabbing our pal's arm, and whisper-yelling "Look, look … boobies!" In addition, a nice butt—sans panty lines—sends us into a got-to-grab-it fit. A reach-around two-handed squeeze is akin to popping packing bubbles. How can we resist?

Taste matters. We're in tough economic times here, ladies. Go easy on the $12 Goose martinis and lobster rolls, will you? This is a big part of the NMB formula because we have to calculate how much it's going to cost us to get, as Steve Harvey puts it, "the cookie" and how much it will cost to keep it. In these tough times, I have developed a keen sense of return on investment in the cookie area. Unlike some of my friends, I refuse to bet on the long shot. You won't see me buying a round of Jägerbombs for girls half my age because I know when I have no shot. A thank-you and a sneer from their faux-hawked baby-boozer boyfriend are all that bet pays off.

Now we have the main factors of the net mating benefit calculation. Massage them different ways and they can result in a hit-and-run or someone worth keeping. A tall thin dummy with huge fake cans drunk on Pabst Blue Ribbon scores high on the get-her-home and get-her-gone chart. A smart sexy little thing that knows her wine and her world news may require a large investment with no return. The average girl with a few extra pounds, a sense of humor, and an awareness of how to ration the cookie to keep us hungry seems to have the most promise.

There's one critical part of the formula missing: knowing what the hell *we* want.

Yes or No

Have you...
Kissed any of your cousins? Yes, one of them in a dirty place: New Jersey.

Been arrested? No, but my mental development has.

Kissed someone you didn't like? Yes, but I was paid handsomely.

Slept in until 5 p.m.? Yes, but I went to bed at 8 a.m.

Fallen asleep at work/school? Yes, zzzz…

Held a snake? Yes, multiple times a day, he's my best friend.

Ran a red light? Yes, I was typing this response in a text message while driving.

Been suspended from school? No, but I tried like hell.

Experienced love at first sight? Yes, every day.

Totaled your car in an accident? No, it wasn't my car and it wasn't an accident.

Been fired from a job? Yes, as an altar boy because I wouldn't put out.

Fired somebody? Yes, because she wouldn't put out.

Sang karaoke? No, I rapped while draped in lesbians.

Pointed a gun at someone? Yes, my handy genetic pistol.

Done something you told yourself you wouldn't? Yes, answered these questions.

Laughed until something you were drinking came out your nose? Yes, and vodka burns.

Kissed in the rain? Yes, it was so romantic filling my lungs with fluid.

Had a close brush with death (your own)? Yes, I dated a Sicilian woman.

Played spin-the-bottle? No, horrors, it would spill.

Sang in the shower? Yes, then the police came.

Smoked a cigar? Yes, and took presidential advice for other uses.

Sat on a rooftop? Yes, but a bird shit on me.

Taken pictures of yourself naked? No, I have an ugly, shy penis.

Smuggled something into another country? Yes, a Russian bride.

Been pushed into a pool with all your clothes? Yes, that's what I told security.

Broken a bone? Yes, fortunately it wasn't mine.

Skipped school? Yes, how else could I have become so smart?

Eaten a bug? No, but I have smoked a roach once or twice.

Walked a moonlit beach? Yes, and I tripped on a horseshoe crab and a vagina.

Dumped someone? Yes, she wouldn't let Dr. Phil examine her.

Let somebody take the blame for something you did? Yes, my evil twin.

Lied to avoid a ticket? Yes, officer I have CP.

Shaved your head? No, it falls out by itself just fine, thank you.

Blacked out from drinking? Yes, wait, what was the question?

Played a prank on someone? Yes, that's what I called it ... she and the judge didn't laugh.

Felt like killing someone? Yes, whoever came up with these questions.

Cross-dressed? No, lace panties chafe me.

Been falling-down drunk? Yes, and standing-up and sitting-down.

Eaten snake? No, I leave that for the ladies.

Marched/Protested? Yes, I was marched into the principal's office numerous times.

Puked on someone? Yes, because she turned on country music.

Seriously & intentionally boycotted something? Yes, church.

Been in a band? Yes, I played flute in an elementary school band. I was twenty-three.

Shot a gun? Yes, it keeps my cats off the counter.

Skinny-dipped? Yes, but it was more like chubby-dipped.

Ridden a surfboard? No, I can fall without the help of waves.

Drank straight from a liquor bottle? Yes, gulp, that's why they make the top fit my mouth.

Had surgery? Yes, I had my faith removed.

Streaked? Yes, and my neighbors called 9-1-1.

Tripped on mushrooms? Yes, I wish they'd mow better.

Passed out when not drinking? Yes, from watching The Bachelorette.

Peed on a bush? Yes, but I wish it was a George Bush.

Donated blood? No, I'm still using it.

Eaten alligator meat? No, just because they eat humans doesn't mean humans should eat them.

Eaten your kids' Halloween candy? Yes, but it wasn't my kid so it was OK.

Peed your pants in public? No, but I promise to keep trying.

Loved someone you shouldn't? Yes, Chrissy Russo, the local meteorologist. But it feels so right.

Think about the future? Yes, lots of hot nights with the woman from the last question.

Been in handcuffs? Yes, I'm actually typing this behind my back in a jail cell.

Believe in love? Yes, and I believe it's made of dark chocolate.

Ever had a one-night stand? Yes, but rarely standing.

Hot Mess

You might be a hot mess if
… you order your next glass of champagne before your last one is finished.
… you do drive-bys past young men to see if they notice your $200 jeans (they don't).

… you admit to having three children, a pending divorce, and a driver.
… you wear makeup to the gym.
… you shop in pumps.
… at dinner you lean into your hot mess friend and giggle, snort, giggle.
… your nose itches, a lot.
… you visit the ladies room more than three times in an hour.
… bartenders know your name, favorite beverage, car, gate code, and the teddy bear tattoo below your belly button.
… your children ask if Dad can pick them up.
… you finish other people's shots.
… you don't get the joke but laugh anyway, before the punch line.
… you sleep in your own guesthouse.
… you get more DUIs in a year than periods.
… most of your male friends are gay and/or African-American.
… your two cell phones (one for family, one for friends) have jeweled cases and taxis on speed-dial.
… you go to the Del Mar Racetrack because they have great Mojitos there.
… your ex-husband's friends refuse to sleep with you.
… your purse is full of personal lubricant and painkillers.
… you have lipstick on your teeth.
… your weave arrives after you do and sheds on the couch more than pets do.
… your mother is a lukewarm mess and your father is M. I. A.

What to Wear

Ladies, please help or don't blame us for looking like tools. We need directions. We don't always read them, but we need them. You can make it idiot-proof like the Coors Light bottle: blue mountains indicate it's ready to drink, you ape.

I have a closet full of options, and I often find myself standing in the middle wanting to bite a bullet and end it all. It used to be so much simpler in the corporate days. A white button-down shirt, black slacks, black belt, black shoes, and any tie will do. Then Mom would throw in a monkey wrench by buying me a striped shirt. I don't want choices, damn it! I want instructions and simplicity. This saves my surviving brain cells for more important decisions, like "Up or on the rocks?"

I'll start at the top.

Hair: I'm going to assume that although there are exceptions to the rule, women do not react favorably to hairpieces, frosting, a combover, hair gel, bangs, and long hair. OK, the last two are acceptable if you are a cougar and he is a surfer and the others are acceptable for your "gay" (noun—sassy male companion who unlike the rest of your male friends is grossed out by the thought of your vagina, knows your shoe designer, and can help with interior decorating). Faux-hawks seem to be in style, and maybe I'm being catty, but they make me want to throw lit matches at them.

Hats: We love hats because we are lazy bastards. There, I said it. What's easier than throwing on a baseball hat, derby, or cap? In addition, it hides those unsightly bald spots and keeps the combover from flailing in the wind, which makes a man look like a sailboat. Crooked and flat-brimmed hats look silly on everyone, including rap stars.

Eyebrows: The caterpillar is not fashionable. I understand that. So, what should we do? Men don't tweeze. If we shave between the brows it will grow back thicker, and boy, is it hard to explain a razor cut there. Men rarely look

WHAT TO WEAR

that closely at our own faces to notice the condition of our brows. I once found a stray long enough to floss with, while connected.

Glasses: Rimless eyeglasses make you look snobby (or stupid, trying to look smart—affectionately called "the Palin"). Thick, dark rims mean you are trying to look trendy, mysterious, and seductive, which all add up to *trying too hard*. Mirrored lenses are out so, unless you're a cop, don't do it. Dark lenses are ideal for scoping other chicks when your woman is in tow.

Facial Hair: I know, I know, the goatee is so five years ago. Tough cookies. What about the rest of it? Does scruff make us look rugged and sexy? Or, does is just itch, tickle, and irritate? Sideburns are stupid and the little gravy-catcher patch beneath the lower lip is disgusting.

Shirts: California is the land of the button-down untucked striped shirt, so I can't wear that. There's also the Affliction and Tap-Out T-shirt craze, which really pisses me off because now that every out-of-shape dork is wearing them, I can't wear them. Those shirts are perfect for me because I'm too much of a pussy to get a tattoo. I'll buck the trend and start wearing white T-shirts and sweater vests. I say, "Bring back the dickey!"

Jeans: No man over eighteen should wear low-riders or cuff their jeans. If you're over twenty-five you're not allowed to have holes in your jeans either. All else goes, but please, men, no camel balls.

Underwear: I get it, no briefs, unless you are at a swim meet. Boxers are fine but they scrunch up when I pull my pants on. Boxer-briefs seem to be ideal, but I find my boys get a bit warm and uncomfortable. They need to breathe. So, what color? Black only? OK, dark colors only.

Avoid anything that might stain or be ready to burn the evidence.

Socks: No socks. What about blisters? I have hairy goddamn ankles, and I'm not shaving.

Shoes: White shoes? Maybe. White sneakers? Hell no, unless you're on a tennis court or in prison. Black sneakers, yes, but only without socks and if you wear white socks, I will throw sharp objects at you. What about flip-flops? Thong-style seems acceptable (except for my annoyingly hairy toes). The Teva-style flops with open toes do not say you are rugged, they say you *take it in the butt*. Did you just say Crocs? I will slap you with a rubber chicken.

Accessories and accoutrements: Watches? Absolutely. Only black, brown, silver, or gold are acceptable. Any other color means you get to do third grade over including square-dancing. Metal bracelets and rings? Why sure, but one at a time there, Roboslop. Cologne? I've heard that real men don't wear deodorant or cologne, they just sweat, and women prefer a man's natural scent. Bullshit. Balls and armpits smell. It is not an acquired scent like eighteen-year-old Scotch. A couple spritzes is all it takes to mask the funk but please don't bathe in it. Wallets? Yes, front pocket only (where bulges belong).

There you have it. Ladies, how did I do? Should I give up, end it all, and let my relatives pick out my final resting suit?

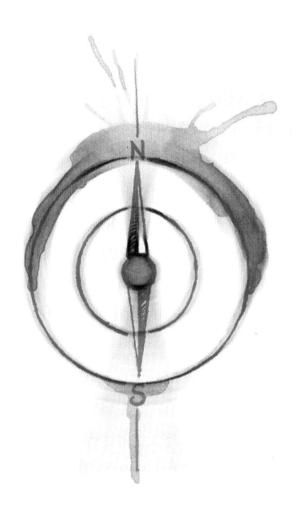

Battle of the Minds

North: She's the most beautiful woman I think I have ever seen.
South: Mate with her.

North: Stop it. Seriously, I know she is too young (according to her), but if she'd give me a chance she'd see that I can offer her more than most men.

South: She's over eighteen, what are you talking about? Can you imagine coming home to her every night?

North: Yes, I can. That's the problem. She just wants to play. I'm not an option.

South: Oh, like *that* has never happened. No young beautiful girl ever hooked up with an older man.

North: Maybe I don't want to hook up. I want her to fall madly in love with me.

South: What are the odds of that? Look around, she has the goods and the options. You need shorter-term goals.

North: But I'm so much more mature now. I know how to protect and provide. I don't need to be out loading up on Red Bull, vodka, and bar sluts. I'd be the perfect stay-at-home man.

South: All right there, Mr. Sparks, drop the romance. Here she comes and she appears lovingly intoxicated.

North: Oh my god, she *is* here. My chest actually tightens when I see her.

South: Try not to look desperate, lonely, and almost fifty, will you?

North: I'm not any of those. I'm a kind and gentle friend always there to listen and support.

South: I think I just puked in your pants. You have one objective, Romeo: Get 'er done.

North: Holy crap, what did this girl drink? She's the hottest walking Long Island Iced Tea I have ever seen. She's totally flirting with me, leaning into me, and touching my arm …

South: Calm down there, Sparky. Play along. She has girlfriends close by so you are under surveillance. This can be good. Future prospects abound. We're working on street value here.

North: What? Look at her. Those prospects are not even in the same solar system. Note the olive skin, dark eyes, and a perfect smile. She's so smart and mature for her age too.

South: And don't forget the all-important silky smooth and toned legs, and if I'm not mistaken, isn't that a hint of cleavage?

North: No, I shall not look. If I look, she'll see me looking and think I'm a pig like the other bar stooges. I'll look directly into her eyes. Just … there.

South: She's ordering another drink. Time to step on the gas. You are now in a race with the alcohol to see which takes advantage of her first.

North: Hey, mister, there is no taking advantage. I'm a gentleman. Maybe she really likes me. Or maybe it's just the alcohol talking. Tomorrow she'll wake up and won't remember any of this.

South: Exactly! So get her home and naked, slay her sexual desire, and don't leave any evidence.

North: I'll do no such thing.

South: You said it yourself, she probably just thinks you're a nice guy, and she's drunk and maybe she could use a little safe loving tonight. She may enjoy it and begin calling you all hours of the day for a little rendezvous.

North: No way. If I hook up with her, she will hate me. She may even call the police. I'll be ruined. I'll be considerate and drive her home safely. She'll appreciate that. Maybe she'll fall in love with me and travel the world by my side. I'll be her knight.

South: She wants you to take her home, throw her on the bed, and show her you know your way around a woman's body, not Venice.

North: She trusts me, that's why she let me drive her home and is inviting me in.

South: Oh no, she is going for more wine. Block it or the only thing you'll be holding is her hair while she vomits.

North: I would do that. I would absolutely be right there with her and do that. I would clean up after, hold a chilled washrag on her forehead, and lay her gently upon her bed. Then I'd kiss her temple, wish her goodnight, and quietly let myself out. My overwhelming acts of kindness would return to me in the form of decades of love and affection.

South: Will you at least undress her?

North: No!

South: What if her dress accidentally hikes up a little?

North: I'll divert my eyes and pull it back down immediately.

South: Do you know how uncomfortable it is to sleep in an underwire bra?

North: I'm *not* removing her bra. Not listening to you … la la la … leaving now … getting in my car … la la la … loud Metallica, need loud Metallica!

South: Just for that, I promise you one performance-anxiety-driven wet noodle.

Expectations

I met a woman who recently had a breakup with her man of six months. He cheated on her and by the end of the night I knew why. Within ten minutes of our discussion, I understood exactly what she had to offer, and what it was going to cost. She's late forties and lives with roommates.

OK, times are tough so I can understand that. She made it clear with all the name-dropping that she expects to be taken care of.

Now, as a man, I have the natural instinct to take care of a woman. I'm inclined to do so subconsciously, and I'm comfortable in the role. My problem is when it's expected. Isn't it easier to manipulate men with fake appreciation than excessive expectation?

If we're walking out to my car, even as friends, I will open the door for you. Will I ever forget? You bet. Most of the time I *will* open your door. But, if you say, "You know, last time you didn't open the door for me and I feel that you're taking me for granted," you have placed a demand on me that does not sit well. Yes, I'll probably open the door for you the next time. Then, when we get home, I will feed your dog chocolate and laugh while it soils your carpets. Wouldn't it be much better to say, "How can I be so fortunate to have one of the few remaining true gentlemen? I feel like a princess when you hold the door for me, and it makes me want to jump you right here in the parking lot." Training successful.

I had an ex-girlfriend scold me once. We were walking down the sidewalk by a street with diagonally parked cars. I happened to be walking on the storefront side, so instead of simply guiding me across to the street side, she said, "A true gentleman never lets a lady walk on the street side of him." This made me want to push her into traffic.

Back to Miss Hand-Out. The discussion covered three topics. First, how odd it was that her last two boyfriends both needed "blue steel" to perform. I didn't find this odd at all. They both must have needed antidepressant burritos to deal with her expectations, thus deflating their libido as quickly as their bank accounts.

Second, she didn't understand why the recent boyfriend had an aversion to oral, both ends of it. That's not something any man would turn down, unless she was a little rough with his soldier on a previous attempt. As far as giving goes, all we need is a little feedback, and we're all in. Lay there like you're having your teeth cleaned, and indeed, next time we'll pass.

Third, she knew this rich dude who screwed an entire fleet of professional cheerleaders, was three inches shorter than she was, and, *ding, ding, ding*, was willing to fly her all over the country to make her his personal pincushion. Now, I'm not saying this girl was flirting with me or had any intentions in that area, but could she make herself any less desirable? At this point, I knew what the net mating benefit was, and it was definitely in the red.

It's so easy to manipulate men. If you like, need, or want something, simply begin with "I love it when you …," "It makes me so hot when you …," or "I bet you can't…" They are all sure winners that we'll jump through hoops to fulfill. If you feel tempted to start with, "Why don't you …," "A gentleman would …," or "How come you used to …," don't do it. You'll turn us into contrary little children because no matter how old we are, that part of us never goes away. Nya na nya na doo doo. Sorry.

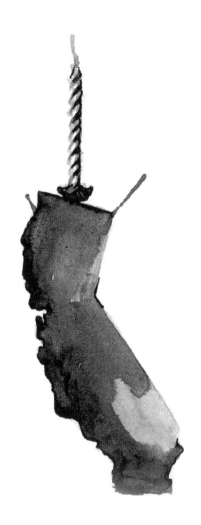

Happy Anniversary to Me

I have just passed my five-year anniversary here on the West Coast. I knew it would be a major lifestyle change going from rural eastern Pennsylvania to southern California, but much of it was unexpected. If you're looking to escape excessive rain, lightning, snow, ice, potholes, gnats, and humidity, here are some observations I have about southern California:

- People are happier and less stressed out mostly because of the weather. I think it's also due to smoking weed and pounding ecstasy like Altoids.
- Bikers are all over the place, and I hate them all. Nothing is worse than sixty-year-old men in tight biker pants, multicolored racing shirts (as if they would have a sponsor), geeky helmets, and clicking tap dance shoes. I want to run them over.
- Almost everybody surfs, and if you don't they can't understand why. I'm not a good swimmer and sharks like Italian food, so I'm out. Besides, they aren't so much surfing as they are floating in little Batman suits anyway.
- Men touch each other too much. There's excessive man-on-man affection in the form of hugging, chest bumping, arm grabbing, shoulder slapping, fanny patting, and leaning against one another. I need personal space with the only exception being boobs: the female variety, please.
- Flip-flops go with everything. I have even seen men wearing them with hooded sweatshirts, slacks, and sweat pants. I can't get used to seeing shaven toes and corn-chip toenails.
- They put avocado on everything.
- People are starving for attention. There are so many "look at me" antics going on that I feel inclined to wear dark glasses and headphones 24/7. Valley girl screeches, obnoxious laughter, and excessive use of the word "dude" all contribute to the circus.

- People still drive like asses (i.e., slow drivers in the passing lane, skidding on wet roads, merging onto the highway driving 30, and being completely oblivious while on the phone). The difference being that other drivers don't remind you as often here in the west. I still use my East Coast training with classic lines including, "Are you kidding me?", "Have a clue!", "Oh, I'm sorry, this is your road, excuse me for intruding!", "Get off the damn phone and drive!", and "You dumb (expletive)!" I also make less use of the middle finger and more use of the what-the-fuck (arms raised, palms up) gesture.
- The women are hot, expensive, and usually willing to put out by the third date (second, if they are married).
- Mexicans do all the work for the lazy white man.
- Fans of professional sports go to games to socialize. Most of them have no clue what teams are playing. It is also acceptable to wear the opponent's colors and cheer for them. In Philadelphia, you would have mustard dogs thrown at you and even elderly women would kick you in the gonads.
- Women dress up to go grocery shopping (thank you very much).
- Botox is so rampant that I can't tell if I have offended someone or if they have gas.
- People love doing dangerous things, including falling from planes, hang-gliding, swimming with sharks, running marathons, skateboarding, and hiking in barren desert areas amongst snakes, scorpions, huge spiders, wild animals, and loose boulders. I'll pass.

- People booze it up every night.
- Networking is more about finding out what people can get from you. I call these people "one-way motherfuckers." When they ask what I do I usually answer "coroner" to end the conversation.
- Women hate every woman they don't know who is dressed nicer, in better shape, has larger boobs, or has had more plastic surgery than they have.
- Women hang with other women who are close to their level of hotness. We had a lot more Abbott–and-Costello pairings back east (I'm well aware of the silly '60s reference). We used to call it "jumping onto the grenade" or "taking one for the team" when offering to entertain the chubby chick while your pal reels in the hot one.
- On most blocks, you can find a Starbucks, sushi restaurant, dry cleaner, hair salon, and a shirtless fat man jogging.

I think I'll sign up for another five years to become fully acclimated. Pass the sunscreen, guacamole, Cabernet, and condoms.

Married Women

Whether a woman is married or not, I'm flattered when she expresses interest in me. It is an uncomfortable pleasure, though. I'd liken it to throwing a brick through your TV. It feels good when you do it, but you know there's bound to be a big mess to clean up afterward.

I can't speak for a woman's sex drive, but I'm aware of the peculiarity of the male sex drive. Once the mental stimulation begins, our thinking becomes foggy. Then as it builds, we become less concerned with the long-term consequences and more anxious for the short-term pleasure. Then, during the act, we pretty much lose all sense of future. Once the deed is done, we have a strange mechanism that makes us lose our desire for fifteen minutes or so. Biology ingeniously built that into us, so we don't continue after completion and scoop out our deposits before they can find the egg.

We typically follow this progression:

- "I would never sleep with another guy's girl."
- "I would never sleep with an engaged woman."
- "I would never sleep with a married woman."
- "I would never sleep with a happily married woman."
- "I would never sleep with a woman whose husband can kick my ass."
- "I would never sleep with a woman whose husband I met."
- "I would never sleep with a married woman I have to see again afterward."
- "I would only sleep with a married woman if I was also married."
- "I would only sleep with a married woman if I didn't know she was married."
- "I would only sleep with a married woman if she was extremely hot."
- "I would only sleep with a married woman if I was drunk."

- "I would only sleep with a married woman if *she* was drunk."
- "I would only sleep with a married woman if I was lonely."
- "I would only sleep with a married woman if she wanted to sleep with me."
- "I would sleep with a llama if nobody saw me do it." (Sorry, I went a bit too far.)

We've all been cheated on and yes, it hurts. It's primarily a pain in the ego. We can't understand what that other person can give our partner that we can't. Well, that's simple: variety. At what cost? Well, it all depends on how far the stimulation has progressed and how likely we are to be caught.

You're probably thinking that I'm a womanizing pig. No, I'm just being honest, and I have learned how to head off this progression to avoid staring down the barrel of an insecure husband's gun. Just because some woman tells me she is on her way out of her marriage doesn't mean her husband agrees. I'll flirt with the best of them, but I make sure she's not into me enough to start the train a-rolling. If flirtation crosses into temptation, I pay my tab, head home, and take care of things more safely (I subscribe to the Playboy Channel).

I'm going to avoid the word "never" because that just tempts nature. At least I have almost mastered my favorite credo, wisely handed down by Clint Eastwood: "A man has got to know his own limitations."

Home Wrecker

Why would a woman have an affair with a married man? It is almost as hard to get into a woman's mind as her Joe's Jeans, but I'll try.

The biggest difference I see between a man and woman in this area is that women usually need more of an emotional connection for that physical connection to work. Honestly, men need a lot less. You can get to men through our eyes. Access to women is through the ears. Women are definitely more attracted to power and mystery than men are. Powerful women usually intimidate men, which is silly when you think about it. Maybe the new breed of cougars will train the young bucks to understand that strong women can still be sexy.

When I was married, I did have an occasional temptation. I was a nightclub disc jockey for twenty years and owned a restaurant and club for ten years. That put me in various situations that attracted women. I was in control of the party, in the spotlight, and gave the impression of wealth. Everyone thinks club owners make a killing. The only killing that is really going on is the slow suicide from the stress of it all.

There was always alcohol around, and I got cuter with every drink. Most of the women who approached me were not interested in having me as a long-term mate. I knew that, and in some ways that made it more tempting. Men don't mind being treated like meat (or tofu, in my case). To a married man, women with short-term goals are much safer bets.

So, what are the goals of a single woman going after a married man? That's a tough one. I can't understand how an emotional connection can come about without the woman thinking, "If he is willing to cheat on his wife with me, who's to say he wouldn't cheat on me?" It gets more confusing when the man has a family. He is willing to jeopardize (emotionally and financially) all he has built. He is showing exactly how committed he is to his commitments. Yet, the woman is attracted to him.

Maybe that's part of it. Maybe the woman feels extra special precisely because he's willing to lose it all for her. Is he really willing or just telling her what she needs to hear? I bet it's more often the latter. We know the way to a woman's heart is through her ears so subconsciously we'll take that route. How often does a man leave the wife and kids for "that girl" and how often is "that girl" left to realize that the role she played was backup sex provider?

I know there are women looking for a quick fix with the married man and nothing more. They enjoy the little flings and are fine in their role. It's like babysitting a puppy: fun until the puppy becomes a dog (burden). These rare women get spooked if he mentions leaving the wife and sometimes they're being vindictive: looking to prove a point.

In summary, it takes two to tango. Everybody has a different moral compass so it's difficult to generalize based on gender. In my experience, if your needs are being met at home, the flirtation won't progress to temptation, no matter how flattering it is. If your needs are not being met at home, having an affair will probably fix that by leaving you with an empty home.

Letter to Myself

At birth: Dear baby Phil, nice ears and fur. What the fuck? Don't let anyone put anything sharp near where you pee and enjoy the boobs while you can because you're going to have to wait another fifteen years to grab one.

At age 6: Dear little Philly, don't be shy or embarrassed to ask the teacher to use the little boys' room. It is a lot worse to sit in your own excrement. When you get sick and someone wants to give you this tasty pink liquid, spit it out. It is tetracycline and it will stain, costing you thousands of dollars for veneers when you get your adult teeth.

At age 9: Dear clueless Phil, no, girls do not have cooties and although being mean to them makes them like you now, keep it up and you won't have a prom date and may end up cutting monthly checks to a greedy ex. Try writing love notes instead of throwing gum at girls' hair.

At age 11: Dear Phil who just discovered his penis elasticity, yes, it's supposed to do that.

At age 13: Dear Phil with the unwelcome hard-on in math class, do not go to the board. Tell the teacher you ate too many sugar babies, have a sour stomach, and will likely vomit if you stand up. Meanwhile, think about Grandma's hairy chin.

At age 14: Dear polka-dotted Phil, quit picking your damn zits. Stop masturbating so much and go buy some Clearasil. No, you won't go blind or get hairy palms, but if your parents catch you, it will mean years of expensive sessions with a therapist who will laugh about your case with his peers.

At age 15: Dear fashion-blind Phil, bell-bottoms, platforms, and Indian jewelry necklaces are not cool. Go buy some T-shirts and baseball caps.

At age 16: Dear deflowered Phil, no, you are not in love. You are having sex and you suck at it, so practice and do it with more than just one girl. Older women are preferable.

At age 17: Dear Dutch-boy Phil, your haircut is stupid. Cut it and put it in a bag for use later when you go bald.

You're not big enough to play football so don't bother taking protein pills or doing squats. In fact, you'll never get paid to play sports so stay on the computer. Your Computer Science teacher will not show you her boobs or sleep with you, so quit staring.

At age 18: Dear alcohol-poisoned Phil, put down the Riunite wine and start smoking weed, you pussy. No, it's not a good idea to drink a pint of kamikazes while camping. Oh, and your Volkswagen Beetle is cool but the color orange is not.

At age 20: Dear Phil the waiter, learn the come-hither and proper oral methods for giving girls orgasms. Black beauties make your heart race because they are not good for you. If you want to stay up drink some damn Starbucks. Oh, that's not available yet? Try Maxwell House then.

At age 22: Dear career-guy Phil, you don't want to be in management. Just keep coding and DJing and buy stock in this little startup called Microsoft with your extra dough. For fuck's sake, *please* move away from the snow and ice already. I don't care if you have to live in a closet with three roommates.

At age 23: Dear romantically-blind Phil, snap out of it. You do not need to get married to have lots of sex. Return that diamond ring immediately and buy more Microsoft stock. Owning a club is a real bad idea so stop thinking about it. Starting writing shit down so it doesn't give you a headache when you're old, trying to remember how much of a mess you were.

Battle of the Genders

Women have to endure the pain of childbirth. Men get to witness the carnage done to their favorite playground (yes, the va-jay-jay) and then play a secondary role to a runny-nosed runt for the next eighteen years: an expensive role at that.

Men have sensitive testicles, which when struck sharply result in excruciating pain, fetal position, and nausea. After bike riding for any significant amount of time, said testicles also voice their displeasure. Shaving the area is quite a chore. Imagine rolling a prune in cat fur and then trying to remove the fur without piercing the fruit's skin. For women, shaving takes two swipes (except for Italians and Greeks).

Women get a monthly friend, which often comes with mood alterations and cramps. Men spend one week a month saying, "What's wrong?" and getting, "Nothing," tears, and nights on the couch as a response.

Men can never hide their arousal. Women often do (at least I hope they do, or I'm real shitty in the sack).

Women have boobs, which come with issues. They must be the right size with just enough sag to hold a dollar bill but not enough to hold a roll of quarters. They should be purple-vein-free, unless nursing. Nipples are very important. They must be between a silver-dollar and half-dollar sized with tips no bigger than a pencil eraser, evenly spaced Montgomery glands, and a reasonable contrast color to rest of said breast. Men have sensitive nipples too but look like silly dinosaurs playing with their own.

Women have to assemble themselves with gadgetry and accoutrements, including creams, makeup, sprays, and hair irons. Men get to read magazines while taking a dump.

Men have to compete with other men in sports. This can include betting, vicariously participating by screaming at their kids and referees, and playing coach from the La-Z-Boy while scratching themselves. Oh, I almost forgot that one: balls itch. Women have to look better than other women (who are all trampy sluts with over-dyed hair, excessive plastic surgery, and fake designer purses).

Women get paid *$dick* for doing the same work a man does, much better than he does, while putting up with unwelcome advances by married upper managers, who all seem to be in the process of leaving their wives. Men pay in the end.

Men are stuck paying the tab for dinner, cocktails, movies, child support, alimony … Christ … why don't I just list what men *don't* pay for? Um, Massengill. Women are tired of explaining that payment does not guarantee entry.

Women are slower runners, can't lift as much weight, and can't jump as high. Men are stupid.

I call it a draw.

The Lover You Won't Fall in Love With

They're safe and perfect for you because you're not ready. You don't want to fall in love with someone because you're worried about getting hurt. It happens all the time and that little marriage certificate—and the fear of losing half—seems to have little preventative value. He'll cheat.

We'll grow apart. She'll have an affair with her boss. He'll find a younger woman. She'll lose interest in me. Painful, isn't it?

Well, one way to avoid it is to find someone you're attracted to but have no cerebral connection with and hook up from time to time. Then, get yourself some opposite sex friends that you have a mental connection with, convince yourself you're not attracted to them, and forbid yourself from hooking up. Maybe after a few wines you can flirt and make out a little, but nothing more. In fact, someone who's already dating another is a good target because there's less temptation: it's safe.

A woman can find a young fellow who has more hair where it belongs, more stamina, and firmer body parts. Sure, he's still dreaming of being in a rock band (because he is so good at Guitar Hero) and surfing is more important than earning a living, but he fills the need: loveless physical gratification. He's your vibrator and, although he won't fit in your nightstand, it's easier to forget where you left him.

Maybe the married man *is* a better choice. Young boys can become infatuated annoyances. Married men—especially if they have children—are often a safer bet. They have more than just emotional reasons to leave when you're done with them. What happens if you fall in love? Will you know when they're only telling you what you want to hear?

Men have a similar difficult choice, but it takes a lot for us to turn down any sexual opportunity, regardless of whether there are emotions involved. Biologically we have millions of sperm to a woman's limited supply of eggs. We can—and I'm not saying *should*—mate and walk away from offspring. Women can't, so they're more selective.

Even if they're on birth control or beyond the birthing years, women subconsciously act on this level.

The safest bet for men is to be friends with someone we aren't physically attracted to. Then, however, our egos fight back because we want to be seen with hot women to keep up our street values. If we're hanging with ugly Betty, we're seen by hot Barbie as flawed. Another choice would be a good friend's girlfriend or wife. It's a little risky but chances are even if we're tempted (or drunk), her guard will keep us from doing something stupid.

We can find a young girl. They're hard—but certainly not impossible—to fall emotionally in love with. They are attracted to wealth, security, and humor. It all depends on their level of maturity. I find a disturbingly high percentage of mature young women and immature older women around. This drives me nuts. You'd think the older women would be more secure and know what they want. They should be completely willing and able to state their desires and—here's the pinch point—act accordingly. Younger women typically have specific life goals and they are less jaded.

Ah, the silly love games. I'm surrounded by young female friends who I'm hopelessly attracted to. I value their friendship, so I'll keep my physical distance. Who knows? Maybe someone will step up, and I'll be brave enough (or slow enough) to not run away. What an exhausting game to play.

Bathroom Etiquette

Someone has to say it so it might as well be me. I'm not one to shy away from criticism, controversy, or uncomfortable subjects. So, here's your guide to proper restroom etiquette.

Public restrooms:

- Men are not to speak under any circumstances. I'll give one exception: "Call 9-1-1, my penis just fell off!"
- Men are not to make eye-to-eye (or eye-to-unit) contact.
- Men must give a courtesy flush between each dropping and never ask a friend to witness the child you just birthed and named. Take a picture instead.
- Women are not allowed in the men's room, unless doing something naughty (and silent) in a stall with a man. If you find one of these women, do not bring her home to Mother. Instead, start loading up on Xanax and penicillin.
- Women are encouraged to gossip and giggle even between stalls, but it's best to check for shoes under each stall before describing your best friend as a sperm Dumpster.
- Women are not to ask to borrow makeup, hog too much mirror space, or spray anything.

Friend or neighbor's bathroom:

- Men, if you can't remember to put the seat down then sit down when you piddle. If some splashes on the rim, seat, or cat use a little wad of toilet paper and tidy up.
- Men, don't ever drop a deuce, unless an ex-girlfriend was in before you, and you want to blame her for the log cabin you built.
- Men, if you clog the toilet, go home immediately and expect fewer invites.

BATHROOM ETIQUETTE

- Women, try to use less than an entire roll of toilet paper during each visit. You're not cleaning an industrial spill.
- Women, don't leave any wadded-up paper in the garbage. We know what it is, and you certainly don't want a small child to dig around and show the party the bloody little white mouse he found.
- Women, don't touch any of the magazines. They are not for you. No, the scale is not off by ten pounds. That would be the spanakopita and spinach dip you just overdosed on.

How to prepare your bathroom for guests:

- Fill your medicine cabinet with marbles to expose the Vicodin hunters.
- Leave two extra rolls of paper and magnum condom wrappers if there are women coming.
- Leave reading material for men, such as *USA Today*, *Maxim*, or *Manners Monthly*. Poor choices for reading material include the Bible, food magazines, and *Juggs*.
- Put out pump soap. Nobody wants to share a soap bar, even if it smells nice.
- Leave a plunger behind the john.
- Leave a tip basket with breath mints and some crumpled ones as a hint.

In summary, treat the restroom as a peaceful place left similar to a crime scene: with as little evidence as possible.

Speed Dating 101

I tried this when I moved to California. What could be better? I'd meet twenty available women in sixty minutes and then select my favorites. If they also select me, our contact info is exchanged and we move forward. Well, that's how it was supposed to work.

Lady #1: Hi, I'm a divorce attorney.
Phil: Bye.

Lady #2: Hello, I have three children under ten, two English bulldogs, and my ex-husband gets out of prison in July.
Phil: I have to pee, be right back.

Lady #3: I kind of let myself go when I was married. I ballooned up to 225 pounds, but I'm taking yoga and the weight is just melting off. Can you pass the bar peanuts?
Phil: I have herpes. Will that be a problem?

Lady #4: I no speakie goo engrish. Wets make babies.
Phil: *Lo siento. No comprendo.*

Lady #5: I only date men with six-figure salaries, fast cars, and homes with guesthouses.
Phil: We're a perfect match! I work at Jack-in-the-Box and they just promoted me to drive-through clerk.

Lady #6: I know it said ages thirty to forty on the signup, but everyone tells me I don't look a year over forty. Would you like a ride on my scooter, young man?
Phil: Did someone just yell bingo?

Lady #7: My ex-fiancé, Jamaal, plays for the Raiders, and we're still close. Can he come on our first date with us?
Phil: Why sure. Can we go swimming, bowling, and line dancing?

Lady #8: You play baseball? Oh my god, I totally love baseball. I like was totally there when Kobe kicked that football thing totally high and made like almost six points.

Phil: I only play so I can see all the boys in tight pants and pat their fannies.

Lady #9: You're from Pennsylvania? What a small world. I had a layover in the airport there once. Doesn't it snow there? God, only a moron would live there, I don't blame you for moving.

Phil: I'm in the witness protection program.

Lady #10: Oh, so you're Italian? Are you like in the Mafia?

Phil: If my name was Tyrone would you assume I can dunk?

Lady #11: You have cute eyes, so blue. Why are you single? What's wrong with you?

Phil: I have poor taste in women, present company included.

Lady #12: No offense but, do you color your hair? I mean, most men are either bald or gray by your age, right?

Phil: Yes, I added these gray highlights for character. Just wait until you see my balls. Can you say rooster neck?

Lady #13: Do you have any pets? Because I'm like deathly allergic to cats.

Phil: What a coincidence. I'm allergic to people who are allergic to cats. You'll have to excuse me. I'm feeling nauseous and I can feel the hives through my jeans.

Lady #14: Do you come to these things often? This is my first one, so I'm not sure how it works.

Phil: Oh, don't be silly, it's simple. You sit on the face of every fourteenth man and have him guess your weight and astrological sign. Giddy up, sister.

Lady #15: Gross, that last man I sat with totally has ass-breath and a chin implant.
Phil: That was my brother.

Lady #16: Aren't you Stacy's boyfriend?
Phil: Ha, you got me. Don't tell anyone but I'm here for work. I work for a marketing agency, and we're trying to see what single women want and we're including free breast exams. May I?

Lady #17: I usually don't date anyone over forty.
Phil: Perfect! I usually don't date anyone older than your daughter.

Lady #18: I'm so nervous. This is my *fifth* martini.
Phil: Aw, that's nothing. I dropped acid an hour ago, and I think I just shit myself.

Lady #19: I love to cook … *wink wink* … can you handle a curvy woman?
Phil: Well, I did bring my rappelling equipment and camping gear. Let's keep this our little secret, OK?

Lady #20: You're so cute. Can you write about me in your next book?
Phil: Um, thank you and that's probably not a good idea, unless you can't read.

Why I Sleep Alone

I'm the lightest sleeper you'll ever know, which is useful only in the rare case that someone attempts to break into my house and rape me. For the other 99.99 percent of the nights, it sucks.

I have yet to find a woman's bedroom where I can sleep comfortably. Nothing is more important than sleep to me. OK, one thing, but that usually helps me fall asleep. If I don't get seven hours, my brain hurts and my eyes feel like they have Cinnabon glazing. The triple espresso helps but then my teeth hurt, and I spend two hours doing wind sprints to the john.

Here are some ex-girlfriends' bedroom features that I can't tolerate:

- They live next to a highway. How can you intentionally select that as a place to live? I don't care what kind of rent break you get.
- They have a dog that has to sleep in the bed. Dogs smell (fur and breath) and when they get an itch, they shake the bed so much that I get seasick. Nobody wants to wake up to a cold wet black nose, except maybe Kendra.
- They have to sleep with a ceiling fan on. This generates a cool constant breeze, causing me cramps and lower back spasms. The fan always has a balance problem, so it's *tink tink tink* all night long.
- Light. Sleeping is best in the dark, is it not? Why must there be any light? If you have to get up to pee, then turn on the light when you get up. Christ, how hard is it to remember where your bathroom is?
- Water bottles. I understand. You can get a little dry mouth. I realize that drinking lots of water is good for you. Do you know what it is *bad* for? Me! I have to hear you roll over, knock the bottle over, pick it

up, unscrew the cap, suck, gulp, suck, crinkle plastic bottle, gulp, suck, more crinkle, gulp, un-crinkle, sigh, screw cap on, put bottle back, knock bottle over, set bottle back up, roll over, sigh, and fall back to sleep.
- Noisy roommates and neighbors. An exception is if they are attractive, female, and the noise is sexual.
- Fifteen layers of sheets and comforters. There's this thing called a thermostat with which you can set a desired—as opposed to arctic or tropical—temperature. You don't get any Greenpeace points for sleeping with the windows open under enough blankets to compress my lungs and sprain my ankles.
- Pajamas. Women should either sleep naked or without clothing.
- Socks. This is the one and only exception to the previous bullet. Cold feet on my back are cause for early termination.
- Whistle-nose. You know that annoying little gob of snot that causes the high-pitched whistle when you breathe deeply? Of course you don't, or you'd blow your goddamn nose.
- Snoring, gurgling, moaning, and talking. Stop it and get therapy, or I'm going to sleep in my car.
- Dozens of big fluffy pillows, meant to be seen and never slept upon. My neck aches from just thinking about them.
- Noisy clocks. Some even have those clocks that generate white noise. Are you kidding me? Who needs to hear crashing waves and seagulls to fall

asleep, besides a pirate? Even if the clock has a loud enough tick, it can send me into a wide-eyed frenzy.

All of the above have contributed to my unusual knack for sneaking out of a home undetected. Sweet dreams.

Things That Make Me Angry

1. People who refuse to bag their own groceries.
2. People who order salad dressing on the side.
3. Married women who act more available than their single friends do.
4. Skateboards.

5. Bike shorts, shirts, helmets, shoes, and the tools they cover.
6. Back hair.
7. People turning left.
8. Jewelry store security guards.
9. Old men driving Corvettes.
10. Alarm clocks.
11. Sunglasses with manhole-sized lenses.
12. Thinking of something to say after sex.
13. Dog shit in my yard.
14. Junk mail.
15. Doorbells.
16. Advertisements left hanging on my doorknob.
17. Nosy neighbors.
18. Highway entrance ramp meters and people who can't read "*two* cars at a time."
19. Pictures of sexy women with hair hiding their nipples.
20. Twitter.
21. Frosted hair.
22. Hecklers.
23. Stick figure stickers on the rear windows of SUVs representing family members and pets.
24. Hybrid cars.
25. Someone driving a convertible with the top down when it's cold.
26. Button-down shirts tucked in jeans.
27. Spitting.
28. Lipstick.
29. Nose hair.
30. The DMV.
31. Laugh tracks.

THINGS THAT MAKE ME ANGRY

32. The Geico gecko ... actually, anyone with a British accent other than Ricky Gervais and *Monty Python*.
33. Kobe Bryant.
34. A cracked windshield.
35. Meatloaf (both the food and the singer).
36. Hot, unavailable, flirtatious women under twenty-five.
37. Female newscasters with low voices.
38. Bills.
39. Newspapers (that I didn't order) left in my driveway.
40. Tiny dogs.
41. Traffic cops.
42. Red wine hangovers.
43. Hair in caught in my throat.
44. Bad teeth.
45. Speedos.
46. Hand dryers.
47. Port-o-pots.
48. Blowing sand.
49. Traffic jams.
50. Low sodium soy sauce.
51. Men wearing jeans with holes or cuffed bottoms.
52. Wife beaters (both kinds).
53. Whiny children.
54. Church.
55. Flies.
56. Leftovers (cold pizza excluded).
57. Shaving.
58. Smoke alarm batteries dying, which only happens when I'm sleeping.

59. Surfers changing their clothes on the street.
60. Loud cell phone talkers.
61. People who confuse *their* and *there*, *it's* and *its*, and *who's* and *whose*.
62. People who pace.
63. People wearing foot thongs with sweatshirts.
64. Hats pulled down to the eyebrows.
65. Anything knit.
66. The marine layer.
67. Reunions.
68. Al Sharpton, Madonna, Glenn Beck, and anything ending in Bush.
69. That Sandra Bullock is married.
70. Sticky movie theater seats and floors.
71. Fortune cookies.
72. Condoms.
73. Water bottles.
74. Martini glasses.
75. Infused vodka.
76. Parking.
77. The word "penis."
78. Pumping my own gas.
79. Getting text messages while driving.
80. News.
81. Showers (bridal, baby, and rain).
82. Buffets (except Jimmy).
83. Gifts (buying, giving, and receiving).
84. Store clerks who say, "Can I help you?" when I'm just browsing.
85. Waiting for my latte.
86. Zoos.
87. Excess tattoos.

88. Lip, nose, and eyebrow rings.
89. BMWs.
90. Asian drivers.
91. Gardeners looking in my windows.
92. Leaf blowers.
93. A peck on the cheek.
94. Trying to figure out which handshake to use.
95. Public hot tubs.
96. Waiting to get off a plane.
97. The smell of most taxicabs.
98. Pet fur on my clothing.
99. Playing baseball with old men who still think they are going to be discovered.
100. Writer's block.

Conversations with My Little Friend at a Wine Bar

Me: Cool, there are seats at the bar.

Willy: Leave at least one seat on each side of you open in case a hot chick comes in.

Me: I want to drink wine, but I'll look gay. I'll order a Coors Light.

Willy: Drink wine, you idiot, this is a *wine* bar. Just don't hold it by the stem. You can share it with someone special. Who cares what other people think?

Me: Here comes another striped-shirt dude. Oh shit, he's going to sit next to me.

Willy: Tell him you're saving it. Wait, then when nobody shows you'll look like a lonely loser that was stood up.

Me: I know I don't have any messages, but I'll check my phone anyway, to look important.

Willy: Surprise! You do have some. Too bad you don't need V1@gr@ and penny stock tips.

Me: I spy two lovely women at 8 o'clock. No rings, fit, and good teeth; they could be breeders.

Willy: They are no doubt in the midst of man-hating dialog.

Me: Maybe I'll just make some idle conversation, like "Hey, did you guys go to the festival?"

Willy: You'll get the stink eye. If they wanted men around, they'd be with men.

Me: Oh, here goes the striped-shirt clown approaching them. Watch him crash and burn.

Willy: Wait a minute. They're talking to him. They must feel sorry for him.

Me: I think they're flirting with him. Damn. Why didn't I wear my striped shirt?

Willy: They're just being nice. Striped shirts are stupid. Scout for other women.

Me: Look, there's a cute one across the bar. I'll make eye contact then look away shyly.

Willy: That shows weakness, you tool. Make eye contact and smile. Confidence, young Daniel-san.

CONVERSATIONS WITH MY LITTLE FRIEND AT A WINE BAR

Me: Never mind. She's with that guy who just sat down next to her. I'm better looking than he is … I think.

Willy: Well maybe he's just her friend. Don't toss in the towel yet.

Me: Wait, here comes a tanned goddess. A little young but wow, Daddy likey.

Willy: And speaking of daddies, here's her sugar daddy right behind her. Christ, is he like fifty?

Me: Hey, I'm almost fifty. But I take care of myself. OK, present bottle of wine and bread pudding excluded.

Willy: You don't want to be a sugar daddy. She's one high-maintenance ride. Keep looking.

Me: Striped-shirt dude just got blown off. This is perfect. If they talked to him, they'll talk to me.

Willy: Hold on. Didn't they just toss him back into the boy-pool? You'd suffer the same fate.

Me: Here's an angle: I'll say, "Don't you just hate it when you want a nice peaceful evening with a girlfriend and the man sluts won't leave you alone?"

Willy: Um, wouldn't that make you simply the next man slut?

Me: Damn it. Hey, look over there: three Rancho Santa Fe women. Lots of Botox, cantaloupe boobs with freckles, and hair frizz. I'm in.

Willy: Don't do it. Three is bad. Even if one likes you, the other two will judge you and talk her out of it.

Me: I wonder if the Padres lost again.

Willy: Snap out of it. This is a mating game, not baseball. Concentrate.

Me: I don't have to pee, but if I get up and walk to the bathroom, I can show off my butt jeans.

Willy: Women don't check out man butt. Or maybe they do. Just don't look over your shoulder or stumble.

Me: How drunk and lazy do you have to be to miss the urinal? Gross. Now I get to stand in piss.

Willy: Just hold it until you get home. Don't touch anything.

Me: OK, one more glass of wine, I'm still under the limit. Maybe I'll just talk to the bartender.

Willy: She's busy tending to the bar, you idiot. Just check for messages again. Dial your voicemail, listen to the "You have no messages," recording, smile, shake your head, hang up, and hope that nobody notices how much of a dork you are.

Me: Wait, here comes another prospect. She's gorgeous. Wow, great eyes, cleavage, and she smiling … at me! She's coming up to *me*!

Willy: Just be nice and move down one seat to make room for her striped-shirt man.

Me: Well, the good news is she sat next to me. The bad news is I get to stare at her back, and she has a wedding ring on. How about them Padres?

Willy: Just pay your damn tab, tuck your tail, and go home before your bladder explodes. Tomorrow's another day for you and the Padres.

No Offense

Add that phrase to the list of things that make me angry. You don't get to decide what offends me. It's like saying, "If this hurts, don't blame me," and then smacking someone upside their melon.

Here are some of my favorites:

"You're so mature for your age."
Translation: "God, I hope I wasn't as childish as you when I was your age."

"You don't look a year over forty."
Translation: "You look many years over forty," or "If I flatter you enough, will you buy my next martini?"

"You're hardly showing. How far along are you?"
Translation: "Jesus, walk away from the buffet, will you?"

"You play softball? That sounds like fun."
Translation: "So you still haven't grown up and waste time on the playground with your drinking buddies instead of being a good husband."

"You're still playing baseball?"
Translation: "Do they allow walkers and gurneys on the field? Men over forty shouldn't wear tight pants, ever."

"That's a healthy dinner choice. How are the salads here?"
Translation: "Thanks for making me feel guilty about the steak I just ordered, you skinny bastard."

"What an interesting shirt."
Translation: "Who dresses you, Stevie Wonder? Don't you own a mirror?"

"Wow, what a sexy dress and I love those shoes!"
Translation: "What a whore."

"He's such a great bartender."
Translation: "I tip him enough to get free drinks occasionally, and more flattery may get me some leftover martini."

"Congratulations on finishing that marathon. Wow, twenty-six miles, that's amazing."
Translation: "What kind of nutcase would abuse their body to such an absurd level? Wouldn't it be easier to just write a donation check and not worry about knee replacements before you're sixty?"

"Oh, you're doing a cleanse. How is that working out for you?"
Translation: "You'll be exactly zero fun tonight and I get to put up with your jealous glares as I scarf down these fries."

"What a beautiful home. Did you decorate it?"
Translation: "You're a guy. There is no way you did this because you can't even match socks."

"I want to introduce you to my friend. She's such a sweetheart and really kind and smart too."
Translation: "I'm really tired of hearing my friend (and you) whine about not getting laid. Yes, she is overweight and a grandmother. Beggars can't be choosers."

"I love my [insert anything of value] and highly recommend it."
Translation: "I overpaid for my [insert anything of value], and I feel extremely guilty, but telling you that would make me feel stupid too."

"He has such a beautiful wife, doesn't he?"
Translation: "How on earth did he land her? Is he rich, hung like a Clydesdale, or holding a gun to her head?"

"It's not you, it's me."
Translation: "It's you."

"So, how's work going in this economy?"
Translation: "Did you get fired or laid off yet? Am I going to get stuck with the tab again?"

"Wow, you really write a lot."
Translation: "Get a life."

Scavenger Women

I met a new breed of woman recently. She stalks your man with the goal of tearing him away from you. The odd thing is that she doesn't want him; she just doesn't want *you* to have him. If he leaves you, she'll lose interest. Her game is over. Mission accomplished.

There are enough single men to go around, so why must she focus on the least available? Could it be that she finds it challenging? Maybe she thinks that drawing a man away from his relationship shows he's willing to sacrifice what may have taken years to build for a shot at the scavenger.

She's easy to spot but I must be oblivious to her, mostly because I stay out of long-term relationships. She'll sit next to your man and try to steal his attention. She'll flirt with her eyes and body language while acting innocent. She'll create some kind of drama to distract him. I can hear the Pussy Cat Dolls now: "Don't ya wish your girlfriend was hot like me?"

It must stem from insecurity. She needs to know that she has options: the more options, the better. What an ego boost to have a man leave his promises for a mere shot at her.

Maybe she's in a place where she is not emotionally ready for a relationship. She wants to stay on top of her game, to be confident that when she's ready she can land the man of her choice. She knows the taken man isn't fully available to her so it's easy to catch and release him.

Maybe the scavenger is seeking revenge for a broken relationship of her own. Maybe her man left her for another woman and she can't get back at him. She'll make one of his brethren take the fall.

It could also be jealousy. She sees a man she's attracted to and is jealous that some other (inferior) woman gets to have him. She wants to prove her superiority and all she has to do is yank him out of his current relationship to reach her goal. She doesn't have to stay with him to prove she's the better catch.

Men in relationships must avoid this type of woman. Men have to see her coming and thwart her advances no matter how tempting. That's not easy. A man's ego can be used against him and is hard for a man to control. Men must recognize the scavenger and consider that the attention she provides is insincere. She'll be much easier to resist.

If you are one of these women, I hope you're aware of the selfish game you play, the emptiness of the fulfillment, and the injury you cause to at least two others. If you're not ready for a relationship then be alone. Don't hold one man's misdeeds against all men. When you're ready, try hunting for fresh prey, not someone else's catch.

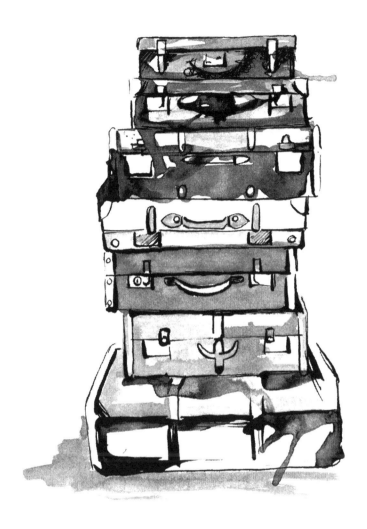

Baggage

We all have it. Some people have more and some baggage is easier to carry (deal with). Let's go through the top ten baggage claims and see how easy it is to fit them into your life, or not.

1. *Smoking.* I don't smoke and the smell of cigarette smoke is repulsive, whether it is coming out of your mouth, nose, or hands. If I pick up a piece of clothing, and it smells like smoke, I'm tempted to toss it. I assume smokers don't realize the stench they carry with them. It sticks to their hair, clothes, and skin. Even if they've recently quit, I can detect it from their lungs during a kiss. Cigars I can deal with because usually they're shared along with the trenchmouth they cause. Pot smoke smells good: *real* good.
2. *The ex.* This depends on how possessive and vindictive the ex is and how much they remain in your person's life. If they recently dumped the ex, then prepare yourself for weeks of drama. Don't make any judgments about the ex because anything you say can be used against you. You say something bad and your mate thinks you're questioning their taste. You say something good and you're taking sides against your mate. Just make sure the ex is not still physically involved (check her cell phone text messages).
3. *Pets.* This depends on the pet and if they are compatible with you and your pets, if you have any. Loud birds should be left outside to play with cats. Little yappy dogs that constantly bark for no good reason (like my neighbor's) drive me to drink. Fat, squat, and smelly dogs, like pugs and bulldogs, are gross and need to live in the yard with a Glade air freshener collar. Big dogs that shed all over me and try to sleep between us need to live with your ex. Cats I can deal with,

because I have two. Any other pet is either a rodent or a reptile not to be owned, unless you are running a Vietnamese restaurant.
4. *Children*. Kids can be bribed. My advice is to part with some green immediately. Bring gifts over, offer to take them to dinner, play catch, and help with their science projects. Give them something their parent wouldn't, like candy, wine, or fireworks. Getting the kids to like you is a top priority. If they don't, you have no chance keeping your mate or keeping secrets from their other parent. You don't want Junior telling his father that his mother has become more religious since you entered her life because he hears pillow-muffled "Oh God…" coming from her bedroom.
5. *Siblings and friends*. Don't hit on her hot sister, no matter what. That never works out for anyone but Jerry Springer. Be prepared for them to interrogate you. Use all the great witness stand strategies you learned from *CSI*: be brief and vague.
6. *Parents*. Avoid them unless they're buying.
7. *Occupation*. Naturally, this depends. If they're a bartender or server, you had better be prepared to deal with them flirting with everyone, and if they are female, yes, every penis-carrying customer will do his best to buy her naked. If they are an attorney, you had better be an attorney. If they are a masseuse, you have a winner until you realize that she's rubbing seventy-year-old fat perverts with those same wonderful hands. Other professions are acceptable as long as they

don't include people who are younger, hotter, and more available than you are.
8. *Religion.* This is a real stickler for me. I gave up fairy tales, and although I understand why someone has faith, I have to bite my tongue. I once had an ex ask if I'll ever believe in Jesus again. I responded, "Well, will you ever believe in *Santa* again?" That didn't go over well. I can't be going to church when there are numerous things I'd rather do on my day off than be reminded how evil I am. I say be amused by it, ignore it, or leave people alone with their masochistic nonsense.
9. *Living quarters.* I wasn't struck by lightning from the last point, so I'll continue. If they are sloppy and you are neat, game over. If their parents haven't taught them to clean their room, what makes you think you can? If they are obsessively clean (e.g., they ask you to take your shoes off at the door) then you have to decide if showering three times a day, ironing everything, and sex in missionary position only is acceptable to you.
10. *Lifestyle habits, including the gym, yoga, running, biking, and hiking.* If these things are an important part of their life, then my advice is to have them continue those things without your participation. You can sit on the sidelines and encourage them, but inserting yourself would be stressful. Since humanity has evolved beyond cave dwellers, there is as much need for camping, hiking, and sleeping on cold dirt as selecting my mate by knocking her unconscious with a mallet. That's just me. I'm sure Neanderthals would disagree

while they wipe with their bare hands and eat rodents.

This concludes my lesson on baggage handling. The moral is that if they don't fit, it's best to check them curbside. Have a safe trip.

Noassatol: The Next Pandemic

I learned of a new affliction and it's serious. This will cost me an extra fifteen minutes per workout. I'll add lunges. OK, maybe not lunges, they do look feminine. Maybe it's because I'm going from eye level to crotch level. I can't do the thigh machines for obvious reasons: testicles. The leg curl machine makes me look like a cat in heat looking to be mounted. Ugh, what's left? Squats! I'll do lots of squats.

In case you are unaware of this pandemic, I'll tell you what I learned from a pair of women. A kind fifty-five-year-old man made conversation with them, concentrating naturally on the married one. When he offered to get her next wine and walked away, she glanced down and pointed out that the man had "no ass at all." She even added the karate chop visual to demonstrate the lack of proper hind-end curvature.

I'm sure he had an ass; we all have asses. Perhaps his jeans were just a bit baggy. His first mistake was tucking in the back and leaving the front untucked. I'm sure his intention was to show off his glutes (or lack thereof). However, the ladies' impression was that he forgot to tuck properly after visiting the potty. He was certainly old enough to know how to shake and tuck so I'm leaning toward his being unaware of his affliction.

How does Noassatol happen? Butt atrophy. How sad. Will my posterior begin sagging and resemble an old woman's elbow some day? Horrors. I never thought I'd have to worry about my butt. Woman's boobs sag, and that's another reason why I'm glad to be male. But this is worse. I don't get to see my own butt that often, so how will I know when it begins to let me down, and I become "that guy" with Noassatol?

Then again, if Mr. Meltingbutt had worn some properly fitted jeans or just left his damn shirt untucked, I wouldn't be developing this neurosis. I spent the rest of the evening like a straight man in a gay bar: keeping my back to the wall.

The more I hang out with women the more I realize they're almost as superficial as men are. They also said he had "summer teeth": some were there, some were not. What if this was one of the kindest men in history who developed a cure for cancer and fed the homeless? He has Noassatol, so who cares? Everyone knows you shouldn't leave your house without your buttocks. His professional accomplishments mean nothing without his butt.

I'll not have my accomplishments overshadowed by saggy cheeks! I'm doing Kegel exercises while typing this, and I'm going to each lunch off the floor in squat position. My cheeks will remain pert and perky, damn it.

Instant Entertainer, Just Add Alcohol

Alcohol is a recreational drug for me; it recreates situations that I usually want to forget. I established a clear limit for myself when boozing over the past ten years or so. I know exactly how much I can take before my legs go weak, memories fade, and ugly people become pretty. The secret is to spread the consumption out over three hours and keep sipping ice water (or Coors Light) in between.

Isn't it a funny thing the way alcohol affects us? Some people say your true feelings come out when you're drunk. I agree, with one additional feature: those feelings all become exaggerated. This makes for some humorous, emotional, and embarrassing moments. I've learned the hard way that it's much better to be the amused than the amusement.

Here are some of my favorite intoxication highlights:

- *Gravy Leg.* The drunk's motor skills become so impaired that walking or even standing is a challenge. This usually happens one leg at a time so they take one normal step and one flop step, as if they are trying to shake something out of their pants leg.
- *Spilling.* I'm a pro at this. I think I have E.T. fingers. If I can make it through a night without dumping a beer on myself—or some woman I'm about to scare away— it's a major accomplishment.
- *Excess affection.* The good old "I love you, man." This gets interesting depending on the genders involved. Two men and there's slurring, handshake shoulder-bumps, and missed high-fives. Two ladies and it's high-pitched screeching, hand-holding, and numerous team trips to the ladies' room. With mixed couples there is smeared lipstick, PDA, and impromptu arousal.
- *Annoying the bartenders.* The poor lads behind the bar are just trying to ration the alcohol they serve to keep you closer to happy drunk than annoying douche. Once people get shit-faced, they assume that the bartender is their personal servant. It

doesn't matter if he's muddling; you need your Long Island Iced Tea, stat. Yet, he serves you with a smile, all the time wondering how you ever managed to part with those two quarters left over from the $9.50 tab.

- *The late night junk food run*. Only one thing is worse than the damage we do to our bodies with all the booze: 2 a.m. carne asada. After pickling ourselves over the course of four hours, we decide the best nightcap is cheap Mexican food. Then we wonder why we wake up with man-boobs and the runs to accompany our migraine.
- *Frivolous pussy investments (a.k.a. junk blondes)*. The alcohol adds a degree of bravery and disillusionment to the point where we think buying a round of shots for girls half our age will somehow blind them to the fact that we're old and ugly. Girls are usually nice enough—and cheap enough—to accept our generosity and may even flirt a bit to get an extra round. Let's face it though; we have no shot no matter how many shots we buy.
- *The alcohol reduction plan*. Related to the prior bullet, this is drinking someone cute. Every drink you have causes the shorty-two-forty to lose twenty. People you would never give a second glance suddenly become viable mating options. This is how a ten o'clock two becomes a two o'clock ten and an expensive taxi ride.

Fortunately, a good side effect of intoxication is memory loss so you can always say, "I don't remember. I was drunk."

Hair

I just found a hair on my penis.
I'm hoping this won't come between us.
Assuming it was loose.
I pulled but it was no use.
Add this to the reasons I'm spouseless.

Does this only apply to men? I bet if I added up all time I've spent dealing with hair it would be staggering; it's probably more time than I've spent, say, commuting. I appreciate my Italian heritage but have no idea how we evolved to have hair where we do. Fortunately, I don't have a shag carpet back, but I bet I can find hair almost everywhere else.

Evolution should have taken care of it. Men should have lots of hair on their head, some wispy strands on their arms up to the elbows and legs to the knees, and sufficient chest and pubic hair to keep the spouse warm without resembling a Ken doll. There is no need for hair in the following places:

- Nose
- Ears (in and on)
- Between the brows
- Armpits
- Knuckles
- Toes
- Shoulders
- Back
- Butt
- Taint
- Testes

Imagine what we spend on hair products, including razors, creams, shampoo, conditioner, color, clippers, stylists, waxing, hats, hair-ties, and Drano. Why can't scientists come up with a way to wash hair down the drain? This would save me from having my pipes snaked practically monthly. I finish shaving and nearly doze off waiting for the sink to empty.

Hair doesn't gross me out like most people, probably because I'm so damn furry. If I find a hair in my food, I just pretend it's mine, pull, flick, and continue eating. Hair on the soap, however, is disturbing so I use liquid soap.

What really irks me is finding a hair connected where is shouldn't be. I'll be shaving and see a stray twister coming from the top of my ear. That just has to be a loose one or piece of fuzz, right? Nope. I pull and it is connected and uncoiled about a half inch long. How could it have gone unnoticed for a long enough time to grow to linguini length?

Girls have the same problems and maybe even worse ones. They do without shaving their faces but have to do daily leg and armpit work. Some women get the frightful upper lip or chin hair. Women also have eyebrow and lash maintenance that men (other than Adam Lambert) don't. I have found a stray hair on a woman—once or twice on a nipple—causing me to sound like an old Hasidic Jew as I tried to dislodge it from my throat.

Then there's hair loss. I was panic-stricken during my late twenties as my forehead grew. I saw so many bad toupees that I convinced myself it would be all or nothing when that day came before I'd wear road-kill. I guess I could always comb over my ear hair.

Now there's the color: annoying grays start cropping up. They start at the chin and go north and south. Naturally, the grays grow thicker than the browns. I know they sell products for coloring facial hair but mine grows so fast I would need to apply it twice daily.

SUCH A NICE GUY

I swear at times I feel like a Chia Pet. I stand in front of the mirror naked with my clippers and do hands, arms, pits, chest, and nether region. (I learned that—much like a nicely landscaped great oak—clearing the base of the tree provides an illusion of grandeur.) By the time I've finished trimming my hedges, I'm standing in a pile of fur large enough to name as my third cat.

First Impressions

Ladies, what do you think when you first see a man? What do you notice about him? Do you fantasize about being in compromising situations with him? How often are first impressions accurate? Almost never.

I'll give you the man's perspective, starting with my own. Keep in mind that my perspective has been warped by dysfunctional relationships, marriage, and entertaining yet stressful occupations: office geek, waiter, disc jockey, bartender, club owner, and self-employed beach bum.

I first notice the size of the woman. This includes height and width. I know that a taller or heavier woman is unlikely to be a long-term prospect. Tall women don't fit; they give me an inferiority complex. I'm not attracted to heavy women, although they are usually more generous lovers. I realize that I do make a subconscious assumption that big girls are less healthy. I can't even defend it.

Next, I notice hair length, color, and style. I admit it; I'm distracted by blonde-haired women. Naturally, they come with some stereotypes, but I've dated enough of them to ignore those. It is just an initial distraction, not an attraction. Kind of like it would be if they were wearing a small hot pink top in a sea of women wearing black. Longer hair is definitely more attractive, and I'm not sure why. I must have the impression that women with short hair are less feminine and more opinionated and domineering.

Then there are the boobs and butt based on how exposed they are. I'm more of a butt man, and again I'm uncertain why. It could be because boobs all have different levels of sensitivity, so there's more work involved in *involving* them. If there's tight clothing or skin exposed, that will draw my attention. Excess skin exposure signals promiscuity, which can be a good or bad thing depending on my time of the month.

Clothing is important. Color and fit are critical. A woman dressed in all black scares me that she is hiding something. This also applies to loose-fitting outfits. I love a bit of cleavage and tight jeans. If I can see a sliver of light between her thighs when her knees are touching, I find that oddly attractive.

Shoes, bags, jewelry, and nails all go to waste on me. Maybe women buy them for other women, not their men. It's just another way to get attention, from both genders. I guess a similar thing for men would be watches and cars. Most women give them little regard.

Eyes, teeth, and skin are definitely important. Freckles—excluding redheads—scare me as does excess tan; it seems unhealthy and signals premature aging. Bad teeth are a major turn-off. Eyes are very important. The coloring, shaping, and trimming of the brows and lashes contribute, but there's either a sparkle in their eyes or not. It is hard to describe. Some women have it: the ones interested.

I can go through twenty evaluations in seconds to see if she's a prospect. Now, if I could only tell if she's interested in me. I know my evaluation is way off most of the time. Yet, it is difficult to convince women that I'm a psychiatrist (not just a good mating option) qualified to provide an in-depth evaluation. The exam remains brief and superficial until the conversation begins, and that's a whole other story.

Internet Mating

This is not about me and not about any of you. Let's say I made some parts up and other parts are about old friends. I need this disclaimer for various reasons, including covering my butt in the odd chance my book gets so popular that I end up on *Oprah*. I never want to be on the receiving end of "Oh no you di'int" and three snaps on network TV.

My good friend Hank told me about an internet date he had downtown. His date had one of those profiles where every picture was from the shoulder up. Nevertheless, she said she was athletic and fit, so he agreed to meet. She parked at his condominium, and they walked over to a local restaurant. He noticed on the walk over that she must have been referring to football or sumo wrestling when she said she was "athletic."

She had a great personality: pleasant, honest, and not shy at all. The discussion was stimulating (as opposed to everything else). Then she confessed that she developed a bad shopping addiction while she was married, which left her with "huge credit card balances that will take her decades to pay off." Well, nothing says future wife and credit counseling more than a plastic-slinging princess.

On the walk back she asked if he had a hot tub. He found that to be an odd question and wondered where she was going with it, fearing the worst. He pointed out the public tub in the common area, hoping that she specialized in water treatment and was not about to suggest a late night plunge. To his dismay, she suggested a "skinny dip" and then called him a coward when he declined. He politely lied, saying the concierge forbids late night bathing as he escorted her back to her car and bid her farewell.

The next night he met a lively young woman who worked at the zoo. Hank loves animals and tries not to eat them, so he figured she would relate. He was pleasantly surprised when the full-body photos on her profile accurately represented her. He took her to his favorite Italian restaurant and ordered the first round of wine. The conversation was good, the flirtation was apparent, and things were looking up. Then he noticed upon his second sip of wine the emptiness of her glass. This foretold an interesting evening.

She proceeded to lap him twice on the wine circuit, downing four before dessert. She was a relatively tiny thing and began showing the effects quickly. When she staggered off to freshen up, he knew it was time to slow down the alcohol consumption and speed up the mating process. Flirtation increased and turned somewhat physical. He paid quickly and flagged down a cab to try to beat the wine resurrection.

They went up to his condominium and bee-lined to the sack. A woman with few inhibitions (even when alcohol induced) early in a relationship is *muy bueno* … according to him. As they consummated, he carefully watched for signs of impending doom. Sure enough, once he took the superior position, he noticed the telltale sign of sweaty upper lip palpitations. He tried to finish the job quickly but his head was no longer in the game. She sprinted— more like bounced off the hallway walls—to the bathroom and proceeded to give a vocal performance worthy of a Grammy.

All the time my friend Hank just laid there staring at his manhood, which resembled an angry Grinch with a condom hat. "What could I do, Junior? It's not my fault." Junior wanted no part of it. Little Miss Pukes-a-Lot stumbled back, quietly put on her clothes, and asked him to call a taxi. He never heard from her again.

This was just one weekend of internet dating fun for my friend. He has since had plenty of bizarre dates, which have taught me to take down my online dating profile.

The Come On

I recently went to one of the few local establishments that show the Padres' games. I have yet to understand why San Diegans prefer watching surfer videos from the seventies over the local professional sports team. In Philly, this would cause a mild insurgence. Anyhow, while hanging out with a friend, I couldn't help but notice two *chicas* staring our way.

"Don't make eye contact," my conscience (or Jesus) kept telling me. They were both pretty: pretty *unattractive*. I'm sure there are men who would have found them acceptable, but I can't like what I don't like. I can't play pool with a rope.

Well, it was only a matter of time before I accidentally made eye contact. I wish I would have thought quickly and picked my nose. But no, I sat there and volunteered to take what was coming. One got up and approached us. The bad makeup made her resemble an adult version of a baby beauty pageant contestant. She tapped me on the shoulder and said, "Exhuse me, my fren, she like you."

Now, the truthful response would have been something like:

- "Sorry but she's not my type: attractive."
- "Really? Well I no like her."
- "OK, send her over while I get my latex gloves on."
- "How's her veggie lasagna?"
- "Could you have her stand on the bar stool, remove her clothes, and pirouette?"

Nevertheless, I took the route most people would: I lied. I said, "Aw, how sweet. I'm sorry but I have a girlfriend." This is a lie on many levels. First, I'm not sorry. I'm somewhat flattered, but not really. I'm a little offended because I arrogantly consider myself too attractive for her. Second, I don't have a girlfriend (read the rest of this book for reasons why). And last, I'm misleading her into thinking that if I didn't have a girlfriend, I would be game.

She was unfazed by my response; perhaps it didn't translate properly. Her next statement was, "OK, how bout heem?" as she pointed to my friend. He should have taken offense to that because if *I'm* road-kill, he must be uglier road-kill. I was a little upset that she didn't press harder for me and just took the next option. She could have made a case for me to leave my make-believe girlfriend.

"Oh, you see, he has a girlfriend too," I responded kindly.

As she waddled away my friend turned to me and said, "Wouldn't it have been easier to just say *we* are lovers?" Good point but then I bet her English would find new clarity as she blabbed about the two pickle-licking gringos sitting at the bar.

Why couldn't her friend be Chrissy Russo or Jewel? Maybe I just need to work on my imagination and drink more tequila before turning away opportunities so quickly.

How I Love Chrissy Russo

Her sexy lips move and I don't hear a single word she says. Just kidding. Of course I do. I hang on every word. For those of you unfamiliar, she is a talented Fox (the company and the animal) meteorologist. Note that I did not refer to her as a "weather girl" because she is much more than that.

She is my morning pop-tart companion and quite possibly the most beautiful specimen on the planet (*sniff*).

Well, sure, I'm not there actually "with" her, but she is here with me, in high definition. Now, before you begin alerting the authorities let me reassure you that I have no bad intentions and I'm not on any sexual deviant map. (OK, maybe one in Brazil, but foreign countries don't count.) I just want her to have my babies. Is that so bad? I'm not stalking her. I have no idea where she lives. I just look forward to the day when she wakes up next to me smelling of hibiscus and honeydew.

Ah, the 3 a.m. alarm and the bliss of seeing the moonlit outline of her sexy purple teddy as she sashays to the master bath. I can almost hear her humming a tune as she starts the shower: "I will always love you" by Whitney Houston, perhaps.

After her steamy shower, she lotions up, and crawls back under the covers with me so I can lotion those hard-to-reach spots on her back. Then she gives me a five-minute thank-you snuggle. Next, I prepare her favorite breakfast as she selects what to wear from her 400 outfits. Yes, my spare bedrooms were converted into closet space and my cats are none too impressed. Silly felines.

As she puts those final touches on that immaculate body of hers, I slice her grapefruit just the way she likes. All the individual pieces are sugar-dusted little pyramids, so she can remove them with the greatest of ease. I can't have her breaking a nail when thousands rely on her and the climate bows to her every whim. I also prepare her poached eggs and lightly toasted wheat bread with peach preserves. Her freshly squeezed orange juice is waiting as I hear her pretty feet bound down the steps, like Miss America.

She greets me with a reassurance of her love as she turns a cheek for me to plant a gentle and moisture-free peck. (We can't have any foreign substances on those porcelain features.) She sits at the breakfast nook and opens the cloth napkin that I thoughtfully folded in the shape of a funnel cloud. After her sigh, I'm graced with the first forecast of the day. All other San Diegans must wait, but for me, it's a head start. I know to expect 72 degrees and sunny before the common folk have any clue. I'm so blessed.

I walk her out to her car with a freshly made nonfat soy double latte with a single squirt of caramel in her Fox Weather travel mug. I kneel, kiss the back of her hand, and tell her how proud I am of her. I anxiously await her three-hour broadcast and her return to my loving arms. I'm so lucky to have the queen of all high-pressure zones as my morning mate. Actually, I guess I'm just lucky to have a vivid imagination.

Aging

You know you're getting old when…

- You inadvertently mail a letter to yourself because you put the bill in the envelope incorrectly.
- You ask for your tab at a bar after you already paid it.

- You lose your sunglasses … on your head.
- You pick up someone else's cell phone thinking it's yours.
- You lose your keys in your pocket or purse.
- You can't read the menu.
- Your sleep is interrupted by having to pee.
- You forget which gym locker is yours.
- You date someone without realizing you broke up with them years ago.
- You leave your credit card behind.
- You need them to turn the music down.
- People are passing you on the right.
- You try to play a video game with a teenager and get soundly trounced.
- You need someone to show you how to set your ringtone.
- You put the cereal in the refrigerator and the milk in the cabinet.
- It hurts in the morning.
- You forget how to spell a fore-letter word.
- People call you sir or ma'am.
- Getting out of your car requires Houdini's flexibility.
- You consider yoga and golf sports.
- You go to more reunions than weddings.
- Young people showing PDA disgusts you.
- You'll admit that someone is actually too young for you to consider dating.
- You read newspapers at a bar.
- You forget the one thing you went to the grocery store for until you get back home with all the things you didn't need.

Tell Me a Story

My friend's daughter is a brilliant thirteen-year-old. She's one of those kids bored with school because she's not challenged. Like most kids, she loves me, and I must confess that I find it flattering. Kids love me because I'm a good listener. Kids nag their parents so much that the parents tune them out, like an ad on the radio.

I had a funny conversation with her while a group of us had lunch.

"Tell me a story," she kept saying. I asked what kind of story she wanted to hear, and she said, "I don't know. Tell me something funny about some ugly or crazy people." Isn't it ironic that this thirteen-year-old knows my calling, which took me almost fifty years to find? She brought me back down to earth with, "You're old so you should have lots of stories." I never did like midgets, even cute ones.

Sure, I have been in crazy situations with incredibly silly people. I'm not sure those stories are appropriate for a young teenager, but I'm probably underestimating today's youth. I was remarkably ignorant about women, relationships, and sex as a teenager, but I also didn't have answers to the questions of my youth. I couldn't Google "BJ" to learn that it was nothing similar to inflating a balloon, and I had no way of understanding what it meant when upperclassmen called me "Phil McCrackin."

I stalled and wondered what story I could possibly tell her that would entertain without going over her head. I know kids like fart jokes. So, I told her the one about my chemistry teacher. He used to walk out of the classroom mid-lecture for fifteen-second intervals for no apparent reason. One brave classmate finally followed him to see and was dealt a nearly lethal blow from the teacher's hindquarters. I'm sure it was a substance not listed on the periodic table: a recycled combination of stale break room coffee, cafeteria macaroni and cheese, and bourbon. Nothing could have been funnier to Phil at thirteen.

Are the same things funny to both teenage boys and girls? I have no idea. Kids seem to find humor in silly stereotypes and human conditions. The things that she comes out with would land me on the bug-eyed end of Reverend Jesse. She calls two of my closest friends "Chocolate Man" and "Big-Nosed Guy" and I try telling her not to, but I can't keep a straight face. It's easier for me to correct her and say, "Actually they go by Chocolate Thunder and Toucan Sam." Kids do say the funniest things which when uttered by adults become politically incorrect. That's unfortunate.

Finally, I fell back on what I thought would harmlessly amuse my little friend: more fart and retard stories. I can't be faulted for playing to my audience. At her age, I clearly remember my favorite story told by my uncle:

"Once upon a time a dog sat on a dime. The dime turned red and the doggie dropped dead."

I guess you had to be there. I defy you to find a thirteen-year-old who doesn't find that one of the most profound poems they have ever heard. Sorry, I have to go. My skateboarding friends are waiting.

Professing

Why must we profess to maintain our faith? This applies to marriage, religion, and sports. It's not enough to hold a commitment privately. Keeping the faith often requires us to display it publicly. People who don't take a stand are found weak or untrustworthy instead of indifferent.

Let's start with marriage and relationships in general. Men feel the need to profess with statements like "This is my girlfriend" and "'Til death do us part." Steve Harvey wrote about it and he's right. If a man won't introduce you as his girlfriend or spouse and uses your name or "my friend" instead, then he is not committed to you.

Look at all the professing we do leading up to the ultimate professing of our love: a marriage ceremony. We hold hands and place attention-grabbing signs on our territory: diamond engagement rings. Then we publicly announce our engagement, send out wedding invitations, and commit in front of our closest friends and family (and God, depending). Then we celebrate anniversaries as achievements shared publicly to tie the binds more tightly. Do we do this for the benefit of our friends and family? Nope. We do it because public promises are harder to break.

People have a lot invested in their religion, and the public displays of their beliefs make it difficult for the faithful to consider how illogical their faith is. The faithful invest significant time and money in their religion. Catholic schools, books, church dues, donations, and icons all add up. Nobody wants to consider that their tithe simply pays the clergy's wage. They want to know it cements their faith and improves their chances of salvation and immortality.

Are religious people strongly committed to their faith because the words in the Bible (for example) are the literal words of their creator instructing them to be faithful? Why subscribe to that particular religion? Is it because it's the faith their parents introduced them to and the one they invested so much time professing publicly?

People profess faith in the Bible constantly, although I bet more of them have read (and understand) *The Da Vinci Code* end-to-end than the Bible. The Bible is ancient with inconsistencies and outrageous claims including unhealthy views of women, children, and lifestyles. However, instead of scrutinizing and performing historical studies of the texts, parishioners publicly profess their faith in order to remain faithful.

Sporting events are massive arenas of professing. We wear our team's jersey or colors not because we look good in it (except Chrissy Russo in a Charger jersey). We don the colors to show our faith and commitment to our team. There are obvious reasons to support our local sports teams, beginning with supporting our local economy. Yet, we stay committed to a team for no other reason than because it's the team we have always rooted for. If the Yankees and Red Sox players swapped teams, I bet their fans wouldn't. That's because they have professed their support and to switch teams would be hypocritical.

I love to make people uncomfortable when they ask me "Who are you rooting for?" so I usually respond, "Whoever wins." That way I'll never be disappointed.

I'll Treat You

I'm not a therapist, psychiatrist, or life coach. I'm not qualified to give advice on relationships based on any academic training. If you ask for my advice, you had better prepare for self-serving responses instead of a textbook analysis. Yet, I don't need any certificate on my wall to make you feel better.

Past relationships taught me how important listening is to women. The thoughts that pop into my mind when someone is talking (whining) to me include "What's the solution?" and "What more interesting related story of mine can I respond with?" Usually women just want to vent and feel support and compassion. I can do that but it's hard to withhold the solution. Depending on my level of interest and intoxication, my advice can vary.

I'm sure parents get stuck in this trap.

- Kid: "Johnny hit me."
- Dad: "Then hit him back." [Reaction.]
- Mom: "Ask Johnny to stop or he won't be allowed to play with you." [Reason.]

- Kid: "I don't want any more spinach."
- Dad: "Eat it or no video games." [Reaction.]
- Mom: "I bet Johnny eats all his. He's going to grow bigger than you." [Reason.]

- Girl: "My boyfriend doesn't seem interested in me anymore."
- Phil: "Find a new boyfriend. I'm single tonight (so far). Where do I apply?" [Reaction.]
- Phil: "That's awful, you poor thing. You deserve a man who cherishes you." [Reason.]

- Girl: "It's so difficult meeting someone I can connect with."
- Phil: "Are you putting out?" [Reaction.]

- Phil: "You're wonderful so of course you're a difficult match. Don't settle and be patient. I'm sure your prince is on his way." [Reason.]

- Girl: "I gave him my number two days ago, and I can't believe he hasn't called me."
- Phil: "He's probably married or gay or both (depending on the state). Can I have it?" [Reaction.]
- Phil: "I'm sure he's just busy and maybe a little shy. He'll call you." [Reason.]

- Girl: "I'm tired of being single. Men are such players. I want a relationship."
- Phil: "Want to make out?" [Reaction.]
- Phil: "Men are so immature. I wish I could meet someone like you." [Reason.]

- Girl: "I caught my boyfriend cheating on me."
- Phil: "What a scumbag. I hope he skins his knee in a puddle of hepatitis. You should get back at him by cheating with me." [Reaction.]
- Phil: "Well, it's a good thing you found out before you married him. Now you can move on and find the man you deserve. He'll regret his loss." [Reason.]

How did I do? Is it honesty, kindness, compassion, or clever manipulation? I can play the role (and so can you). I consider myself qualified for this psychological dance. It doesn't pay well, but it is easier on the knees.

The Real Housewives of Phil's House

Reality TV drives me crazy. I honestly try to make it through an episode and I only end up feeling disgusted at how fake it is. It should be called "fake TV," not reality TV. It's mostly scripted because if there's not enough dysfunction, there is no entertainment value. Who wants to see a bunch of happy little homemakers in aprons being good mommies?

Here's how I imagine the taping would go at my house:

Phil arrives home from work ... wait a minute, I work from home.

DIRECTOR: "Cut! Jesus Christ, Phil, get out of the damn house, will you? Just put on some khaki pants and drive around the block, then walk in. Here, take this briefcase and travel mug with you."

Phil arrives and walks in. His lovely wife Chrissy is scurrying around the kitchen preparing a fine meal of eggplant parmesan. His favorite Silver Oak Cabernet is poured and waiting as he greets her.

DIRECTOR: "Cut! Borrrrr-ing. Chrissy, we're going to need you to be on the couch masturbating to the movie *300*. Here, add this pot pipe and some Doritos and let's have the Stouffer's eggplant burning in the microwave."

Phil finds his lovely wife flicking her bean and drops his briefcase in horror. He smells the odd combination of marijuana and burnt eggplant smoke. Phil walks back outside and calls his therapist.

DIRECTOR: "Cut! You damn pussy. How about this? Phil, you walk over and take the pipe from your wife, walk back outside, and pee in the neighbor's yard."

Flash forward to the happy couple eating off their laps while watching *Chelsea Lately*. Their teenage son, Barnabus, walks in with his skateboard and friend Johnny.

THE REAL HOUSEWIVES OF PHIL'S HOUSE

DIRECTOR: "Cut! OK, we're going to need ole Barney to walk in with two hot teenage girls in skimpy bikinis. Let's add some interracial flavors. How about one Puerto Rican and one Brazilian? Oh, and lose the skateboard and walk in with a Fender guitar."

The happy couple discusses their stressful day as Chrissy makes the bed and Phil changes into his gym clothes.

DIRECTOR: "Cut, cut, cut! Chrissy, we need you in the bathtub with candles and baby oil. Phil, you stand in front of the mirror and do some manscaping. Then take a picture of your manhood with your cell phone and send it to your boss's wife."

Later that evening, the couple sips martinis at a local establishment with some close friends. They talk about the Padres, their uncontrollable teenagers, and hair coloring.

DIRECTOR: "Cut! OK, let's move this whole party to a dive bar. Phil we need you to hit on the bartender and try to talk her into a threesome. Let's have a second couple fist fight over by the jukebox while a third couple, Phil's grandparents, play beer pong."

Our lovely couple returns home. Phil, being a true gentleman, opens the door for his wife and carries her to their master suite, just like their first night together. They make love in the moonlight.

DIRECTOR: "Cut! I'd rather watch paint dry. Let's have them race to the front door. Chrissy, you trip Phil from behind and drop an elbow on the back of his neck. Once inside, Phil can throw oranges at her. We'll climax with Phil waking up at 3 a.m. to play a prank on his unsuspecting wife by stuffing blue M&Ms up her nose."

    End scene.

Speech Template for the Next Governor Caught Cheating

I have had it with whiny sniveling middle-aged men at the podium apologizing for indiscretions. The latest is South Carolina's Governor Mark Sanford, who spent a week in Argentina and returned to give the anxious-as-always media a tear-filled dose of his lament.

I couldn't make it through his speech because I became nauseated. I'll take it upon myself to write a template for a man's man speech that will be more about the truth and less about what voters need to hear:

Dear fellow Americans, let me start by making it perfectly clear: yes, I *did* have sex with that woman, and lots of it. In fact, I had to rehydrate with two quarts of Gatorade—while I iced down my apprentice—to recover from the many nights of "hitting it" like Albert Pujols.

Those of you without a penis may wonder how I could do such a thing. Those of you *with* a penis just want to know how the sex was; I'll get to that. So, how could I cheat on my wife of twenty years? Quite simply, I did it because the bitch stopped putting out. Tell them, honey. When's the last time *you* headed south? Seriously, she had her day, and she's not bad for fifty. But, after pushing out four pumpkin-headed monkeys, sex has been one-sided; I only feel it one side at a time. It's like stirring warm gravy.

Hey, I admit that I'm not the physical specimen I once was, but I have these things called money and fame that make up for it. Still—and this is for my sons—if Mommy would have hit the lights and backed up to Daddy more often than once a month, Daddy wouldn't have spent your summer camp money on his trip to South America. Believe me, boys, soon enough you'll learn to understand and envy Pop for taking the road trip.

I know you nosy perverts are all getting off on my emails that you intercepted. Well, just so you know, here on my iPhone I have action shots that will make the most timid of you hotter than the desert sun. My little playmate,

Olivia, isn't shy about showing Uncle Mark how she loves Americans. I'll be selling these photos on eBay to fund her summer vacation with me.

You may be expecting an apology. Let me see, do I apologize? Um, how can I put this gently? Hell no I don't! The only thing I *am* sorry about is that I couldn't get a travel visa quick enough to have her here by my side in a crotchless Latina maid's outfit.

I'm well aware that my little trip will cost me dearly in terms of alimony and child support. That's why I'm tendering my resignation effective immediately. I'll move into a studio rental and make my living from appearances and book deals while I continue to bang South American chicks by the dozen.

In conclusion, I'd like to wish my future ex-wife well in Cougarville. All you judgmental, hype-seeking drama queens of the media can "suck it." God bless money, God bless fame, and God bless hot foreign chicks willing to put out for old glory.

More Than Just a Haircut

Men always find wisdom at the barbershop. You women miss so much by seeing stylists. In order to maintain a buzz cut I need to make visits every three or four weeks. For my $15, I get plenty of extras, including eyebrow trims and unsolicited advice.

My Mexican barber asked how my Father's Day was. When I hesitated, he said, "You know, you seem like the kind of guy that can't be bothered with children." That was perceptive of him.

I asked, "What gives you that impression?" He said I don't look stressed out enough to have bambinos, and for that matter, I must not be married. That was another good call.

I confirmed that I do enjoy my freedom. He said, "So, who cheated, you or your ex-wife?" I acknowledged that I was indeed married for thirteen years, but we had an amicable parting.

He laughed, "Yeah right. You cheated, didn't you? I'm not judging. It's in our nature as men. Women have to understand that." I love the way he found me guilty by association. By not denying anything, I was admitting guilt.

"No, seriously man, we just grew apart. We were great roommates but the passion was gone," I defended. He wasn't buying it and steamrolled past my excuses.

"Look, if she cheated on you then, man, you have to let the bitch go. But they need to allow us men certain indiscretions. We think about it all day. So, if we slip up, they just have to understand."

"Really?" I responded.

He said, "Oh hell, yes. If she cheats, then I can't forgive that, no matter what. You ever been with a girl for the first time, and she cries?"

"Well, once I accidentally ... uh ... um, come to think of it, no." I had no idea where he was going with this, but I didn't want to distract him.

"You know why? She cries because you just kicked the man she loved out. Yep, that last guy before you? She loved him and he messed up, so now you're there and she knows she can't go back to him. So she cries because she's sad that she lost her man, and she's afraid that you'll mess up too."

Wow, and all this time I thought she cried because I had my elbow on her hair.

There must be a culture gap here. Is he suggesting that Mexican women allow their men to fertilize any old lawn? They look the other way? Yet, if the women step out of line at all, out they go. That's crazy. I can't respect that. I want my women to have enough pride to not tolerate my doing things that they wouldn't do.

To go along with my freshly shaven neck, I now have the wisdom to recognize the signs. Next time my date cries, I'll be flattered instead of asking for her ID or considering male enhancement.

Friends I Should Leave Home

I'm really not on anything. Seriously. I'm enough of a mess on my own. I don't need any help. If I were to mix alcohol, pot, and stimulants, I bet I would have a lot more writing material. Let's pretend that I ingest all three before heading to the wine bar this evening with my new friends.

Driving there:

- Drunken Phil—I wonder if I can pee in this water bottle while driving. Come to think of it, why is *that* legal but talking on a cell phone isn't?
- Stoned Phil—Oh my god, that's a cop. Wait, I'm doing forty. Is forty too slow? Phew, it was just a dude on a Harley. I think I have sunflower seeds somewhere. I smell something. Did I remember cologne?
- Pumped Phil—Ha, I'm faster than you are. You suck. Watch this, Mr. BMW. Eat dust. Oh, and your polo and visor look stupid and I hope your head gets sunburn. Golf is for douche bags. Try hitting a 90 MPH fastball, you loser.

Walking into the bar:

- Drunken Phil—I'll limit myself to one glass of wine unless there are cougars. In that case, I'll have two. I wonder if my tongue is purple. If it's all couples, I may just go home and cry.
- Stoned Phil—Wow, did I just drive here? Where did I park? Oh, ha, right there. Silly me. Wait, did I forget to lock my doors? My car is so cute. Oh shit, where's my phone? Whoops, it's in my hand. Mm, French fries dipped in olive oil.
- Pumped Phil—I'm not leaving this place without pussy. I should wear my iPod and listen to Sevendust while I drink Jägerbombs. Maybe I'll do a few push-

ups here in the lot and get my guns ready for action.

While in the bar:

- Drunken Phil—I'm pathetic. The men here are all pathetic. But *they* have women. Damn. OK, more standard-lowering Pinot for me. I will not hook up with an ex. Maybe some bread will soak up this alcohol. Yes, ice water too. There's always Scotch and water. How does it go? "Wine before Scotch, soon a woman's on my crotch?"
- Stoned Phil—I wonder if anyone here can tell how messed up I am. My brain itches. Look at that dude's head. What a bad toupee. I think I see a paw. Wait, did he see me looking? Great, now he thinks I'm gay. I need dessert. Oh look, she's bending over. Crap, is that her father or husband?
- Pumped Phil—I don't need no stinking woman. I'll just high-five these dudes here and try to network. Who needs women anyway? Wow, look at her cans. How I'd love to use them as ear warmers. One more tequila won't hurt. Limes are fruit and fruit is good for you.

Leaving the bar:

- Drunken Phil—I don't know what will make me sicker, the smell of this Armenian taxi driver or the burrito I'm craving. Why does my head feel like a water balloon? I have to pee again. I just peed

- two minutes ago. Well, any bush will do. "Pull over, please." Oh man, I forgot that I have flip-flops on.
- Stoned Phil—Wait a minute, did I pay my tab? Where's my credit card? Did I leave a tip? I bet they all made fun of me when I walked out. Mm, chocolate-covered pretzels. Shit, where did I park? I think I drove here, or did I take the bus? Mm, guacamole with hot sauce.
- Pumped Phil—So what. I'm going home alone because I want to. I could have had any of those women. I just don't feel like it. Just wait until my book signings start. It will be a nonstop vagina parade. I wonder what's on the Playboy Channel.

On second thought, I think I'll leave these three ingrates home, stick with sober Phil tonight, and try to humor somebody into my sack instead.

The Smothering

Sometimes we hold so tightly that we hurt the one we love. It's a delicate dance. I'm into you more than you're into me, but then I pull back, and it switches. For a brief moment, we're on the same affection level but then off balance again. How do I know if the pendulum will swing back my way? When? Why must we play these silly love games?

It's painful to observe, actually. A younger man (thirties) and a recently divorced girl (forties) with young children had a rendezvous near me recently. I grabbed popcorn and some Ju-Ju-Bees and started taking notes. She was anxious for his arrival but when he got there, he smothered her. All I could think was, "She needs a challenge, and this guy is playing it all wrong."

Maybe he was just marking his territory. There were plenty of older dogs present and interested, so he may have felt insecure. Poor puppy. Her girlfriends gave her looks with the odd mixture of envy and disgust. He wouldn't stop touching her hands, arms, and back. "Jesus, dude, let her breathe, will you?"

I know it's important to have your man "praise" you, but can't it be overwhelming when there's an audience? My guess is that, like most marriages, the passion left hers years ago, so this is the medicine she needs. Maybe she's overdosing. I guarantee he'll scare her away. There's no way for her to keep up with him because if she did they'd be going at it on the wine bar carpet.

It's a delicate balance. Take it from an old dog that has played this game enough to know the rules. He should ration his love. Get close, grab her above the knee firmly, and whisper in her ear, "You're so sexy. You're driving me crazy." Then kiss her earlobe, sit back down, and talk to her friends. This plants the seed for later.

I bet he sands the deck during foreplay. Did I lose you? OK, how about this: instead of the entire alphabet he draws too many "I"s? You still don't get it? Jeez. He spends too much time looking for the little man in the boat and chasing him around the lake. Got it? Never mind.

That kind of affection is not something the puppy can sustain. He's not pacing himself. If she gets used to it, he's in big trouble. No matter how many oysters he downs, he won't have the stamina to continue blanketing her. Her friends are letting her slide for now because they know the ex was a real shit and she deserves some passion. Eventually they are going to let her have it. "Honey, a toy like him is fun to play with but a month from now you're going to want to donate him to Goodwill."

It all depends on the situation. I may be selling him short. Maybe he's playing the way she needs him to, for now. Maybe he'll build a wall around her, and then pull back once she's secure. What do I know? I can only observe and be there to pick up the pieces when he breaks her. Patient persistence prevails.

Del Martians

I'm not opposed to cosmetic alterations any more than I'm opposed to new wardrobes. Some people can take plastic surgery too far. I see people with facial distortions that give me the urge to poke them with a stick. It isn't just women. I find it more disturbing to see a man with plastic surgery.

Is it just me? It looks so obvious and unnatural, especially on men. There were six men in their late fifties I saw at a popular beach bar recently. They all had freakish enhancements. I can't be sure what all was done, but their eyebrows were too curved and high, their foreheads too shiny, and skin pink and blotchy. I'm not being catty about it. They looked like they were either recovering from serious burns, or frightened.

They certainly had no shyness issues. They approached all the girls with airs of confidence. That must be the reason. People have work done to enhance their self-esteem more than their physical attractiveness. Women love a confident man. Maybe it would be cheaper for these men to hire an entourage to remind them how wonderful they are.

Does it work the same for women? Women have a lot more pressure on them from society to retain their youthful looks. They have clothing, makeup, and heels to consider. Then they undergo extreme grooming including hair, nail, and skin care. There are nutritional and physical pressures to keep the right curves and tone without any extra bulges and dimples. That's brutal.

It's funny that straight men rarely notice new hair color and shoes, so I assume the women are also doing it for a combination of self-esteem and peer pressure. Women check each other out more thoroughly than men do. Women use their looks in combination with subtle cues to get their man's attention including: skin exposure, hair flips, subtle touching, body movements (dancing), and flirtation.

Yet, many of the forty-plus women at the beach bar needed construction zone signs. Boobs? Of course, and I'm OK with that, even though they are technically just globs of fat. Most men prefer natural boobs, but we certainly will make do. If *you* like them, *we* like them. Botox? OK, this has to stop. I need to be able to interpret expressions in order to get accurate feedback for my advances. When all I can see is a pinched nose, fat lips, and a porcelain forehead, I have no idea where I stand.

It's funny that they haven't come up with a cure for elbow wrinkles and old hands. When I have a hard time telling the generation of the cougar, I look at her paws. What do women look for to determine the man's age? Hairlines? Bags around the eyes? Knobby knees? Tommy Bahama shirts?

If there's something we can do to improve our self-esteem, we should do it. When you're comfortable in your skin, you have a natural allure. A display of confidence is a magnet for women. For men, overconfident women are intimidating, so I suggest showing less arrogance and more skin. Either way, I have a surefire way to improve my confidence and appeal: open another bottle of wine.

The Marriage Lease

I'm not jaded. I had a decent marriage but, what if the rules changed? What if we had new nuptial options? I don't think it's practical to commit to anything "'til death" so let's come up with more realistic ways to wed.

Options are available based upon their ages, their age difference, and the number of previous marriages. All leases come with a one-time renewable option. When a lease is not renewed, the couple leaves with what they came into the marriage with, and splits what they accumulated while married. There is no alimony. Child support and custody are determined as they are today.

Note that nothing in the lease prevents a couple from staying together after it expires. They can both decide to do that; they just won't be legally obligated. There are instant opt-out clauses terminating the marriage lease if either member is caught sleeping with another. If it's just oral pleasure, then there's a lease acceleration clause, which removes half of the remaining term.

The five-year lease. This is the longest lease, and it's available only to first-time couples both in their thirties. Sixty days before the end of the lease, both parties vote to renew the lease for another two years or let it expire. If either dissents, the lease expires, and they spend the last sixty days splitting assets.

The three-year lease with two-year renewable option. If either is under age twenty-five, there is a ten-plus year age difference, or either has been previously married, they have this option.

The two-year lease with one-year renewable option. Available to people divorced more than once or with kids under eighteen from another partner.

The starter lease. This is a one-year lease with a one-time lease upgrade offer to one of the above leases at the end of the term. Designed for people forty and over, this lease provides the most flexibility.

Sure, there may be some discomfort when you have to return your mate at the end of the lease. However, think of all the new models to hit the market that you may want to take for a spin. Make sure to do your research and be confident that the previous owner took proper care and did not abuse them (drive them too hard). What a wonderful way to free up the divorce lawyers to spend more time not being greedy assholes.

The Turtle Always Wins

As we age, men learn to make up for their bodies with their brains. Boys don't see how we do it. They rely on their youth while the old turtles creep slowly behind, waiting to capitalize on their mistakes. Before the boys realize what happened, they're left in a sobbing heap. Good thing boys have quick recovery times.

I play baseball with three groups of men: 18+, 35+, and 45+. I notice the progression from youth to maturity as follows:

- Speed and flexibility go from roadrunner to "Call a taxi."
- Strength and endurance go from oblivious to "Please pass the Motrin."
- Intelligence goes from brazen stupidity to prudence.
- Recovery time goes from instant to "Help me out of bed."

For example, the boys won't pace themselves during a baseball game. The pitchers will just try to blow fastballs (without finesse) past the older men and pay the price. The youngsters can't hit a good breaking pitch and have no sense of when to take a pitch or advance a runner. That's why old dogs can get over on them. We learned pacing, finesse, and subtle ways to exploit youthful aggression.

How does this relate to dating? Boys rarely pace themselves in relationships as well. Three Red Bull Vodkas and they go straight for the clitoris. They hardly have time to take off their crooked baseball cap. Maybe that's why the cougar population is growing. Mature women know these boys will dive right into the deep end without testing the waters. They take less time to think about what they are doing and are less likely to "take a pitch."

The young bucks certainly have us in strength and endurance. They come equipped with less body hair and more abs. They'll seal the deal anywhere you like: front seat, public bathroom, or beach. Old men don't have the flexibility. Sure, the boys finish the game more quickly, but they are ready for another game in minutes. We, on the other hand, usually need a cold compress, some fruit juice, and an hour of TV before jumping back in.

However, the mature men excel at using their accumulated wisdom to leave the boys dazed and confused. We know the right amount of alcohol, compliments, and humor to add to the women to get them lathered up. Boys assume that shots and obnoxious PDA are all it takes. They haven't learned the fine art of listening. No matter the age of the woman, they love eye and ear contact and the old men know exactly how to feign interest.

What about girls versus women? The young girls—in my experience—also rely heavily on sedation. Then again, maybe that's my fault, as I seem to bring the inner Lindsay Lohan out of them. These girls also burn quickly and crash hard so it's a good idea to keep a towel handy.

The most significant difference I have noticed is guilt. Young girls seem to carry a lot more of it around. "I have a boyfriend." "I really shouldn't." "Will this hurt our friendship?" "I don't usually do this." "You don't have anything, do you?" "I've never had a one-night stand. I don't know what's getting into me."

The mature woman grabs you by the ears and asks you to leave before sunrise. They don't want to explain to their children that you are not the new daddy. Yes, there is a price for youth, and I think the key is balance. After two twenty-fives, it's wise to throw in a fifty to prevent burnout.

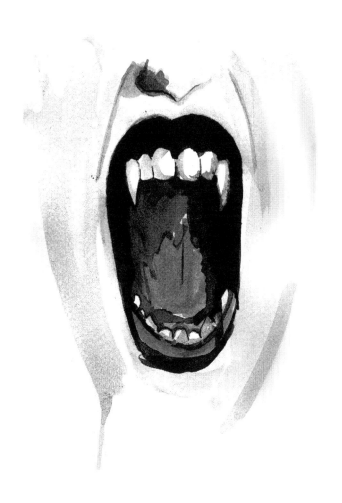

Bite Me

In the past year, we have witnessed an incredible vampire craze. I can remember as a child the thrill and fear of *Dark Shadows*, a daytime soap. I'm sure if I watched it today, it would be laughable. What's the big draw? It must be a generation gap for men. I don't have any male friends interested in vampires.

Demand is created with the combination of violence and romance. Pure violence is boring. It must be the animal desire—the hunger—that is appealing. It's related to an interesting survey I saw in *Maxim*. Most of the women surveyed preferred their sex to be rough and dirty. Forbidden and primitive lust must be attractive and stimulating.

I haven't been with many women who liked it rough—or, so I thought. I'm closer to the gentle end of the scale. I think of women as delicate and precious, to be handled with care. That's how I was raised. My aunts and cousins were always quiet, demure, and pleasant. So, I tend to caress my girl and watch my language.

Yet, I'm seeing growing herds of aggressive women. They're not intimidated or limited by social stigma. These women curse like a sailor: dropping f-bombs without batting an eyelash. I find that a little hot and a little disturbing. I'm not only getting used to it, I'm starting to appreciate it.

With more practice, I think I could do the verbal nastiness thing. Men, though, need to be selective about the dirty words they use. Certain words seem to come out all wrong such as "penis," "vagina," "titties," and "hiney." If I ever let one of those slip, I sound like a third grader. The similar words on the other end of the spectrum are just too extreme for me right now. I'll work on it.

I need training in the physical area. I can't bring myself to be rough with a woman. If I ever bruised a girl, I would be mortified. Yet, some girls love being bitten, not nibbled. I hate being bitten so I can't relate. How can you tell how hard to bite anyway? Should I clamp down until I get kneed in the groin or taste blood? Do you remember the hickey craze when we were young? Girls were proudly hiding them.

I bet that "rough sex" has a wide range of interpretations based on the woman and her experience. Some women might consider it rough enough to have their wrists held; others beg to have them tied. Some might consider it rough to be face down; others can't climax any other way. Some think it's rough if they have a gag reflex; others choke themselves. Some appreciate a firm grope; others leave nail marks.

There's a cerebral thing in play with the whole vampire fantasy as well. The vampire displays extreme desire; they can't live without your blood. It feels good to be desired that much, right? They charm and seduce you and take your innocence. They don't care whose lover you are. The vampire takes what it wants. What will it take to let them have *you*?

Rules for Men at the Gym

I was traumatized last week. I was in the locker room, head down, avoiding all eye contact, and I came within five feet of the most alarming, disturbing, awful sight of my life: a fifty-year-old man with a tramp stamp. I kid you not. I wanted to ask him what bet he lost. What could possibly drive a man to cash in all his testosterone for ink on his lower back?

I'm well aware that I'm no fitness model. Hence, I wear appropriate gym attire, which doesn't include tiny tank tops and Speedos. I love to get an early sweat going in the sauna next to the pool. That's where I find disturbing slingshots, nut sacks, and sausage casings.

Have they no dignity or mirrors? There is no reason to wear a tiny little nut-sack in a public place. No one is trying to shave seconds off their 100-meter time. Girls cringed in discomfort and I almost puked in my mouth at the site of masculine cellulite and gray strays surrounding the grossest of all swimwear.

Here's another thing: there is no reason to be naked in a public locker room for more than, say, five seconds. Towel off in the shower stall, wrap the towel around your waist, and head directly to your locker. Put your damn boxers on first. I don't care if you're eighteen or eighty. Nobody wants to see a turkey-neck anywhere but in a soup kitchen.

At my last gym, the *coup de grace* was so horrible that it will be difficult to put into words. It disturbed me, forcing me to find another gym. Our locker room had one of those hotel-style blow dryers, normally used to dry *hair* on the *head*. I came around the corner to find a 5'6" sixty-year-old pudding of a man standing naked with legs akimbo, literally blow drying his nether region. I could clearly see the pubes tumbling through the air in slow motion like the club in *2001: A Space Odyssey*.

Why? Why not just towel off? Does the hot air feel good? OK, maybe it does ... *but not in a public place.* Men are so messy down there anyway in comparison to women. Female privates are neatly tucked away. Men have their frank and beans plus skin folds best left unseen. Few straight men appreciate anything about another man's body. Women are a different story. Women can appreciate the breasts, hips, butt, skin, etc. Men have nothing worthy of a comment such as, "You know, Don has such nice skin. I can tell he does a lot of lunges, keeping his buns plump and firm."

I want rules. Gyms need to forbid hairy-backed and hairy-shouldered men from wearing wife-beaters and grunting on the bench press. Wearing Speedos should be as illegal as wearing cellophane. Anyone caught naked in the locker room for more than fifteen seconds is an *exhibitionist*. They should be sprayed with foam insulation and kicked to the curb.

Barriers

We all have criteria about what is an acceptable date and mate. I know there are some things I need out of a partner and some things I'd never live with. Maybe we become fussy. If we tempt nature by saying, "I'd never date someone who...," aren't we setting ourselves up to be tested?

I understand this all changes depending on your current life situation. Your age, career, family, and environment all drive your requirements. Past relationships weigh in as well. We learn what we can put up with, and what we can't tolerate.

Let's take the case of the single woman in her thirties finding herself with the naturally increasing urge to have children. They're out in increasing numbers because most are getting married later in life. Women are more career-oriented straight out of college, delaying the breeding. When breeding time comes, these women have some real tough decisions to make. One of them is whether to involve a man at all or hire a sperm donor. They must have major trust issues to consider that route (plus a large bank account and an *au pair* or two).

If a woman is looking for the father of the child she wants to have soon, what does she require, other than his fertility? He must share her intentions about how to raise the children. That's a tough one. I see three primary factors involved in the equation and I'll call them the three F's: Fitness, Food, and Faith.

Fitness is very important. Unhealthy parents set bad examples for their children. Does the prospective father overeat, smoke, or drink heavily? How often? Does he have a family history of cancer or heart disease? Is he athletic? Do you want your children to be athletic or do you prefer artistic? Do women think of all these things? How do they know for sure that the man is being honest about his fitness?

Food determines fitness, but I'm mostly concerned with food choices. In my case, I don't eat meat and haven't for ten years. I chose to stop eating meat because, in my opinion, it's an unhealthy food choice. I don't care what other people eat. I prefer that my mate educate herself about her food, and if she does and still craves the weekly juicy grilled steak, I can live with it. That's what I want for my children. I want them to make informed choices as soon as they are capable.

Faith is definitely a showstopper, which I find unfortunate. Jews and Christians expect to share their faith with their mate and children. I understand why: their parents taught them what is acceptable. Some people of faith find it hard to believe that a person without religion can have morals. That's a cruel and uninformed prejudice. Atheists value life—sometimes more than the faithful do—because of the preciousness in the finality of it all. Why don't we expose children to various faiths including the option of living without religion? Let them make an informed choice, as they eventually will in deciding their political affiliation.

The best option is sharing the goal of raising a happy family and concentrating on the goal instead of plotting the exact path there. I'm not the same person I was years ago. I change, my preferences change, and my lifestyle changes. If I try to pave a nineteen-year path to parenthood, I can't see how it would end up anything other than frustrating. A more realistic goal is, "Today I desire to meet the person that will exceed my expectations as a lover and parent: a friend who will inspire and support me in my pursuit of happiness." Isn't it better to have options than barriers?

Ex Games

Explain to me why so many people hate their exes. For ex-spouses the only plausible reason must be poisonous lawyers. It boggles my mind how you can despise someone who you so recently pledged your exclusive love to, for life. We get hurt—or, I should say, egos get damaged—when the one we love makes what boils down to a change in preferences. I know that sounds sadly shallow, but isn't it true?

People tire of the relationship and decide to move on. You may cringe at this but hear me out. What else in life do you cling to in spite of discomfort? I'm not still wearing bell-bottoms. I don't have sideburns. I don't drive a Le Car anymore. I have no wide-collared silk shirts or platform shoes. I don't drink Zima. Most importantly, I don't eat scrapple. Why? Well, I don't like them anymore (*not* because something is *wrong* with them). My preferences have changed.

Sometimes we make a mistake (to err is male) and return merchandise we should have kept. I once sold Amazon stock and bought Enron. I'm similarly confident that I broke up with women prematurely, not giving the relationship a fair chance. It's easier to deal with (emotionally) when we're the one walking away, so usually I'll run at the first sign of danger. That's unfortunate.

Doesn't it sting when a mate selects another person over you? Think about it, though. Is she choosing another person or another relationship? Hasn't she simply changed her preference? I prefer a white sedan now instead of black SUV. If he leaves a relationship, it doesn't imply that his mate is flawed. There's nothing wrong with a black SUV. He didn't intend to hurt his mate. He made a selfish choice. Seeing it this way may help reduce the sting.

As we accumulate exes, there can be the added stress of running into them. There's a mental struggle because you recall the relationship, weigh it against your current one (or lack thereof), and consider giving it another go. We do this because we're lazy and it's convenient. We already made the investment and played the courtship game so most of that is avoidable. We can skip right to the good stuff. But, if the relationship didn't work before, why would it work now? Well, people change, but not that much. Chances are it would fade as quickly as the sexual afterglow.

At least you should try to maintain a cordial relationship with the ex. It makes everything else less stressful. You don't have to run when you see them out. The pit you feel in your stomach is so much softer when you see them with their new mate. If you can work the relationship back to a non-physical friendship, then you might be able to trade the stress for happiness. It is possible to be happy without being jealous, if you can get to this point.

In the name of lowering blood pressures and dating friends of the ex, let's all learn to not take it so personally. It's just mating business.

The Chase

I'm tired. The courtship game is nothing short of exhausting. Maybe that's why some people get married: they tire of chasing chickens around the coop, and settle. Sometimes I wish there were arranged partnerships.

Maybe we all should have our own Bachelor/Bachelorette shows forcing us to pick a mate and deal with it.

Part of the reason for my frustration is my age. I feel physically capable but I get mentally exhausted quickly. In my teens and twenties, I would relentlessly chase a girl I was obsessed with. Now, I show interest, but if they back off or want to be chased, I sit back down and order another Pinot. Don't women find it exhausting running away, looking over their shoulders, hoping the man is following? Can't men show sufficient interest without chasing?

Here's how it often plays out. I see a girl across the bar that I find attractive (the girl, not the bar: they are all attractive). I look her way and smile. If she returns my smile, I know to assume the three-point stance.

By the way, I can detect the difference between a cordial smile and a welcoming smile. The cordial smile comes with confused eyes saying to me, "Aw, what a nice cute guy. I wonder why he's staring at me."

The welcoming smile says, "Hmm, he's interesting. I wonder if he's single and potty trained. Let's see if he's brave enough to come say hello."

After the welcoming smile, I'll trot over to start the interview. Yes, an *interview* is exactly what it is. I go through my résumé of being divorced, not gay, married thirteen years, no children, two cats, and list my strange occupations. If they don't excuse themselves, I get to hear their résumé. As they go through their traits and desires, I mentally grade each one, similar to counting cards.

- "I love baseball."—Plus five.
- "I have three children."—Minus three.
- "My children are older, not living with me."—Plus three.

THE CHASE

- "I love cats."—Plus two.
- "I'm allergic to cats."—Fold.
- "I have dogs."—Minus two.
- "I'm going through a divorce."—Minus one, hopefully.
- "I have two roommates."—Minus two.
- "Let's grab a bottle and go make out."—Double down.

Then the obligatory phone number exchange and good-bye hug take place. I can tell from the hug how fast I'm going to have to run after or away from them. There's the shoulder-only touching one arm pat with one arm covering breasts, with optional air kiss. That's not a good sign. Then there's the two-armed, chin on shoulder, kiss on the neck, with pelvic connection hug. That's yummy. It signals that a slow jog should be all that's required.

I bypass the whole twenty-four-hour wait nonsense for correspondence. I usually will text them within minutes, to leave little doubt of my interest. If that intimidates them, then I know this is going to be a marathon instead of a sprint, and my knees can't take the pounding. Some girls prefer a phone call and most of the time they'll just let it go to voicemail. Then I feel like a struggling stand-up comedian holding a conversation with myself. "Um, hi, this is Phil, the guy from last night that you met, and we talked. Remember? I know I have a weird area code. That's because I'm from Philadelphia. Ha, get it? Phil from Philly. So, I just wanted to say 'hi' and see if you would like to maybe have a drink sometime. Yeah, so, um, call me back if you want to. OK? Thanks and talk to you soon. Bye."

That's awful. I'll stick to writing because I can do that chase with my mind and my fingers.

All Ears

I have heard it all before, but I keep listening for something new. Sure, the names and ages change, but it seems every woman I meet has a story I've heard before. There are children, pets, ex-husbands, monetary problems, job changes, and trust issues. All I can do is fake sympathy while I look for an escape route.

Who will listen to me? By the time the first "I" comes out of my mouth, I can tell by their reaction that they are still in venting mode, and I'm the recipient. My conscience says, "Why fight it?" and off I go with the free, unrewarding therapy session. I do care about people, mostly for selfish reasons. I want to be surrounded by shiny happy people. Don't we all?

I'm genuinely interested in people. I'm just tired of the ordinary. How cool would it be to meet someone with a unique story that doesn't include some ex treating her like shit, the smartest kids in the world, and a rewarding career? Oh, what I would give to meet a girl that cheated on her boyfriend, smokes weed, and wishes she never had children so she could maintain a hard body and get a full night's sleep.

I have no problem exposing my flaws. Do you know why? Because you're going to get to know them soon enough, so why hide them? I even round my age up. I lie to spice up the conversation. I confess to my obsession with knees, owning a pet armadillo named Cushie, and low blood pressure. They all elicit confused looks and amusing responses.

What am I supposed to do? I have that *inviting* look to me, for some reason. Actually, it isn't *some* reason. I know the reason. I'm quiet and content being alone. That confuses and attracts people. I'm not a West Coast look-at-me person. I'm the man in the corner that everyone wonders what's wrong with. They approach my kind smile and big ears and think, "Father Phil will do just fine for my next confession."

I'm glad they can't hear the words streaming from my conscience. That would be embarrassing. When they say they feel bad, sad, or lonely my inside voice sarcastically says, "Do you? Do you really?" I know it's mean, but I can't control that inside voice. I can only do my best to keep it *inside*. At times I want to paintbrush slap them (extend hand, bend at the wrist, forehand, backhand, and repeat until whining stops or security comes). I feel like grabbing them by the shoulders and shaking brusquely while saying, "Snap out of it, you whining heap of self-important flesh. At least you don't have ass cancer. And if you do, please allow me to apologize for my tasteless humor."

Before you decide to nominate me for mean person of the year, please understand that I'm usually kind enough to listen without judging. It's not easy, but I can do it. I find it rewarding to help people who truly need help but I have become so cynical that my bullshit meter is highly sensitive. I prefer my wine with sharp cheddar instead of the "h."

Office Olympics

I haven't worked in an office full-time since 2004, but boy, do I recall how crazy it was back at the cubicle farm. There were foul bathrooms, office love affairs, and stale mugs of cheap coffee. There were worthless meetings, posturing peers, and narcissistic bosses. It was all so overwhelming. I often envied the *Office Space* worker who sat in an isolated area away from the game, looking for his stapler.

The most frustrating part of my day, especially once I entered senior management, was sitting through meetings. It took me back to elementary school. I was usually so bored that all I wanted to do was read *Mad* magazine and shoot spitballs. Meetings with the top executives were the most painful. I recall a Napoleonic executive who had his own special chair with a hidden button he could push to summon his assistant. His assistant's duty was to bring him a fresh green tea in his special mug every fifteen minutes. For lunch meetings, his lunch of lightly grilled chicken breast was off limits to anyone else; we got pasta salad.

I had another boss who summoned a peer and me to his office and scolded us for misbehaving at a meeting. His daily meetings were full of chest-pounding ingrates. I distinctly recall one clown saying, "I have three reasons why we should employ this strategy. Number one … I forget number one, but number two …" How in the hell do you forget number one? Wouldn't you just make number two number one and forget number three? What a jackass!

My humor got me into deep water at the office. Similar to the kiss-ass meetings were lengthy chain emails. All the little minions felt they had to add their two cents. They each replied to all with, "And my comments are below in [pick a color]."

I was so irritated with email quilts that I responded, "My comments are below in white." My phone rang three minutes later and Napoleon summoned me for yet another reprimand.

Then there were the proximity and privacy issues of the cubicles. One neighbor had a sinus drip problem and

OFFICE OLYMPICS

would snort (and swallow) all day. I could hear it over the music in my headphones. Gross.

We all know that stale cheap office coffee causes unbearable gas. That was dangerous for the office because naturally someone would come visiting seconds after I let one fly, with nobody around to blame.

People decorated their cubicles with family photos to make them more homey. I was so irritated that I once drew penises and mustaches on them after working late. It was my first artistic foray.

Office romances are always fodder for gossip and entertainment. Managers were warned not to dip into the corporate ink, but that is like telling a child not to eat the cookie dough. I spent more time with office babes than my wife so there was constant temptation. We heard rumors about people hooking up on top of the hated boss's desk, in the corporate lot, and even janitorial closets. I found what I think were butt cheek prints on my fine mahogany (OK, particleboard) desk once.

We had departmental sporting events. That gave us the rare opportunity to take shots at hated peers with no consequences. I recall a day of events that included a joust with padded sticks and helmets. We had women go at it so fiercely that I found myself semi-aroused. During a tennis event, I won—in spite of my lack of tennis skills—by playing with my shorts pulled up under my nipples. Distraction kills and nothing is worse than camel balls.

Ah, fond memories, none of which leave me with any desire to return to the office. I do miss seeing the skirts, but I find the drama as repulsive as that tuna croissant I left in the department refrigerator for a month.

Pockets

We used to call them "sugar daddies" but I prefer this new term: pockets. There is a new crop of women in their forties that are reentering the mating market with new strategies. These are not your typical cougars out looking for some young beef. These women give their husbands the heave-ho, add a little facial-filler, and head to the places where the men with deep *pockets* hang.

I don't know which society frowns upon more: the woman seeking the sexual pleasure she's been missing (cougar) or the woman who can put up with unfulfilling sex if she's pampered. I don't have a problem with either. I envy that they have the choice. If I went looking for pockets—at a convalescent home, at my age—I couldn't fulfill my end of the bargain to gain access to the Black Card.

If I can't look for pockets, then I may have to be the one with pockets. Better yet, I can be the one who they *think* has pockets. If I'm going to have to pay anyway, I can play the game. I know one strategy the pocket-seekers have is to check out the man's shoes and his watch. No problem, I can maintain one pair of Prada shoes and a Rolex. Next is the car. A one-night rental or limousine takes care of that. I can drink eighteen-year-old Scotch and even use a fake British accent.

The women deserve it. If they are willing to look the other way while some beer-bellied sixty-year-old plastic surgeon removes their clothing with Veuve Clicquot, then they deserve it.

Men with pockets are well aware of what's going on. I doubt any of these pockets think they're buff enough to land the looker, so they know exactly how to grease the wheels. They promise cocaine, exotic trips, fast cars, and jewelry with the goal of getting the girl naked. Do you think these men have any desire for deep conversation? Hell no. They just want to figure how much it will cost to have her *act* physically turned on by them. It smacks of prostitution, doesn't it?

I heard an unhappily married woman say, "I shop because I'm miserable." In that case, a pocket will do more to satisfy her than a young stud. On the other hand, if she found a man capable of bringing her to climax as well as Ruth's Chris, maybe she'd spend more time in the sack instead of Saks? Maybe the ideal situation is a combination of both. She can play the cougar to fill the baby-maker, look for pockets to fill the closets, and never the twain shall meet.

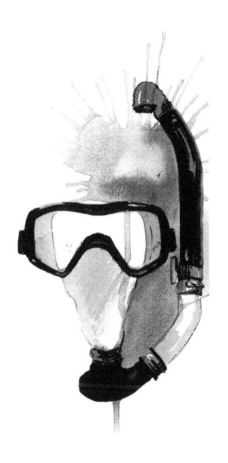

Puddles

Female ejaculation: fiction or elusive fact? I don't admit to knowing, but I do have a friend (we'll call "Hank") who claims to have seen such a beast. When I relay this story, I get a range of responses based on the listener's gender. Men give me the wide-eyed *Three Stooges* responses: "Yes? Yes, yes? Yes, yes, yes?"

Women either say, "Yeah, she's peeing, you idiot," if they are non-squirters or, "Hmm, I never heard of that. Interesting," if they are.

Hank described the elusive animal as a woman normal in almost every way. She was tiny, mid-thirties, with a lap dog, and was never married (clue #1). The only quirk he spotted was her constant need to have a bottle of water (clue #2) nearby. He assumed she simply wanted to stay hydrated.

After a few dates, the couple made their way to her bedroom. She made it clear that they could get naked and fool around, but there would be *no penetration* (clue #3). He assumed she had her monthly visitor, which he could respect and avoid. Interestingly enough, though, she was indeed into manual stimulation as she immediately assumed the gynecologist's chair position, and placed his hand on the faucet.

He said he has above-average skills in that area. His girl was writhing with pleasure, so he assumed that he was talented, she hadn't had it in a while, or he had a hangnail. As she was peaking, he was mentally high-fiving himself. Then she arched her back and there was an audible *pfft, pfft, pfft* sound coming from below, like a lawn sprinkler. He didn't know what that sound was, but before he could check for evidence, she flipped him onto his back to return the favor.

While she reciprocated, Hank nearly dislocated his arm trying to reach the evidence to see if it really was what he suspected. It distracted him to the point of almost being unable to finish his part. Hank said he needed to know so that she didn't one-up him in the sheer volume of ejaculate. After he finished, he reached down and found a puddle the size of a medicine ball. Hank was proud to realize he had just found the elusive squirter.

Being a man of good humor and realizing her obvious discomfort with the situation, Hank decided a witty line was in order to disarm the situation. He smirked and said, "So, I guess if I ever decide to go down on you, I'd better have snorkeling equipment handy."

Puddles was none too impressed. She gave him a look reminding him of his immaturity and said, "Help me change the sheets." Poor Hank never got up the nerve to call Puddles again. That's too bad. I think she'd be an ideal lover because, for one thing, she'd never be able to fake an orgasm.

Sounds That Hurt

I'm overly sensitive to noise. I wish I could disable it. How awesome would it be to mute certain sounds? Having sensitive hearing helped me to become a decent disc jockey back in the day, but now it only seems to raise my blood pressure and cost me sleep. Am I a freak?

Here is my list of most irritating sounds:

- *Leaf Blowers*—They should be outlawed and ceremonially compacted. Whatever happened to the rake? Nothing is worse than having my sleep-in day interrupted by the 8 a.m. blower.
- *Garbage Trucks*—I realize it's a thankless job and someone has to do it, but can't we make them any quieter? Maybe we can force the collections to happen in the afternoons and early evenings. The slamming of the cans and the Dumpster and the backing-up warning beep kill me.
- *Dogs Barking*—That's why I have cats. This serves no purpose except to ward off a burglar, and that is so unlikely it makes the barking unnecessary. I want to invent a high-pitched inaudible-to-human device that I can turn on to annoy the dogs when their yapping starts.
- *Teenagers*—Yes, I'm the grumpy old man. "I was like, and he was like, dude, and then OMG, she was like you know as if, gnarly." Such witty dialogue makes retroactive abortion something worth considering.
- *Train Horns*—Trains are loud enough to make the horn blasting unnecessary. Anyone who can't hear the train coming and is hit is doing the species a service by not passing on their genes.
- *Country Music*—Even if the singer is hot, I can't make it through an entire song without my ears bleeding.
- *Obnoxious Female Laughter*—This is also called cackling. It's nothing more than a look-at-me

strategy for a woman who would be much better served by employing her plastic surgeon and pumps.

- *Inappropriate Applause by Patrons*—I never understood this or what the origin could be. A bartender or server drops a glass and idiots decide it's appropriate to cheer. Why? What if a tendon is severed, crippling the worker? This, to me, is grounds for immediate removal and a public flogging.
- *Dubbed Laughter*—I don't need someone to decide for me what is funny. If I find a situation or dialogue funny, I'll laugh. This is why I can never make it through a sitcom.
- *Obnoxious Fans*—I'm all for people supporting their team. Encouragement is a good thing, but please don't yell anything like "You suck!" at the athletes. No matter how poorly they perform, they are infinitely more skilled than the fans.
- *Snoring*—My own snoring wakes me up, so why do I need someone else's?
- *Snorting*—Gross.
- *Loud Music from Others' Headphones*—If you are so deaf that you need to have the music in your headphones turned up loud enough for others to hear over their conversation, you need a hearing aid (and a slap).
- *Whiny Kids*—Parents have learned to tune them out, which I admire and understand, but they need to realize the rest of us have not. Buy the damn kid his ice cream for our sanity's sake, please.

- *Athlete Interviews*—The grammar used by most athletes reassures me that they belong on the field, under a helmet, far away from microphones. "Now dat's what I'm tawkin' 'bout, G."

I'm sure there are more but it hurts me to continue thinking of them. Perhaps the hearing loss caused by all the George Thorogood and Cheap Trick concerts back in the day will come in handy soon.

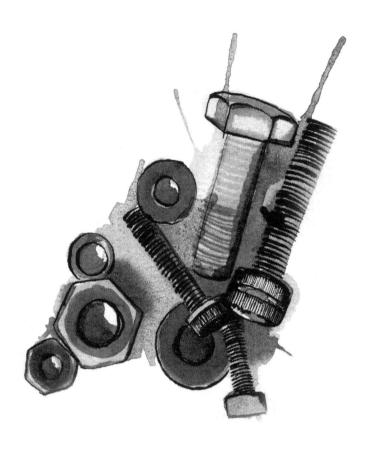

Nuts and Bolts

"So you can make me cum, that doesn't make you Jesus." That's one of my favorite Tori Amos lyrics. It strikes a chord with me about how we'll stay in a dysfunctional relationship because the sex is good. Many relationships have emphasis on one or the other. Either the relationship is wonderful but the sex unfulfilling, or the sex is mind-blowing and the relationship is shallow.

Sex is a critical part of any relationship. I thought that might change as I aged, but no, I have to admit that it's still a deal breaker. Can we all really be that different? A method that works for one should work for all, shouldn't it? If you've seen one you've seen them all, right? Wrong. It appears that the more difficult (deviant) it is to receive pleasure, the more you are willing to compromise the rest of the relationship when you find it.

One of my first loves out of college was a Sicilian girl. She rocked my world but was borderline schizophrenic. Guess what I did. I asked her to marry me. How crazy is that? The week I proposed to her, she became angry for no apparent reason (this happened a lot) and threw a hairbrush at me. Sicilians are known for being ill-tempered, so I shrugged it off.

I look back at that relationship and try to understand what she did that was so wonderful that it had me completely ignore the other twenty-three hours and fifty-nine minutes of the day. I'm not sure. I recall that when she was in the mood, she was *really* in the mood. Her hunger for me was nothing less than addicting. Her personality changed when she was turned on. She became this primitive creature, like a vampire, that desperately needed something I had. It's nice to be desired, isn't it?

I've had other relationships with an intellectual connection but the physical part was clumsy and awkward. Even when I gave and asked for directions, it all seemed robotically forced and scripted. Nothing is more frustrating. It's hard to find someone intellectually compatible. When I do, I expect to be disappointed. What's the alternative?

I'd have to maintain two women: one for physical pleasure and the other for mental stimulation. That would never work.

I wonder why we attract these situations. It should be simple and natural to attract a mate that fits both ways. I hate settling. For men, part of the issue is our natural attraction to younger girls: ones better suited for reproduction. Younger girls are typically less experienced (we like) and less skilled (we don't like). Older women are more skilled and more comfortable giving directions. Nature is throwing us into a conundrum. We search for the older woman with a hot young body and the younger girl with experience and maturity. Both are elusive sexual saviors.

I guess it's better to have one or the other, than neither.

Temptation

How do you handle the stress of discovering a rare connection with a person unavailable to you? There's a familiarity, making you feel like you knew him in a previous life. Or, maybe something about her reminds you of former lovers. When this is one-sided, there's no need for concern, unless an unhealthy obsession develops. When the feeling is mutual, it can be gut wrenching.

If you both know you have this connection, how far do you go to see if it's worth pursuing? Chances are that it is purely a surface attraction. You don't know the other person well enough to know what you want from them. It reminds me of a line my friend said when I pointed out a gorgeously unattainable woman: "Just remember, somebody somewhere is sick of her shit."

Depending on how difficult a match you are, and how dysfunctional and unfulfilling your current relationship is, this can be tempting. I've been there, and I became both frustrated and angry as my conscience fought my desires. I wanted to be with her badly, but I knew the consequences, although remote, could be devastating to my relationship or even my physical and mental health.

The first situation—where both people are in committed relationships with others—is the most perilous, yet the most rewarding in many ways. If the connection, desire, and consequences are mutual, I think it's easier to take that step. Apparently, both parties are in unfulfilling relationships and both consider the possibility of leaving them. The risk is mutual. Yet, there is double the danger of being caught while trying to decide if the risk is worth the reward.

If the man is available and the woman is committed, a different dynamic is at work. There's bound to be some jealousy over her husband, even if she insists the passion has left her marriage. That can cause some discomfort as his feelings grow and he begins to seek ways to wrestle her from her commitment. What happens if the husband finds out? That adds physical retribution as another side effect worth considering. How do we know if the marriage is mutually failing, or if she is just appeasing her new man?

If the man is married and the woman is available, it plays out differently. Men and women do have different moral compasses and consequences to consider. The married man knows (and maybe this will change someday) that he could be saddled with a financial burden as a result, so there is significant risk involved. Men are typically in a position of power and I have witnessed some masterful manipulation used to satisfy their sex drive. I hear that women typically have the same drive, but I haven't seen it. I know how compromised my morals become when I'm aroused. I'm confident that women are better suited to control themselves in that state.

Regardless of the situation, there is a nature versus conscience struggle brought on by this. Nobody is going to make the right decision every time. Sometimes it's worth the risk of causing short-term pain for long-term gain. If we stay in fulfilling relationships and leave the rest of them quickly, maybe it reduces the temptation. If that doesn't work for you, please at least be respectful and avoid getting caught.

Such a Nice Guy

No, I'm not. Well, I'm not *that* nice. I'm still a man with my caveman desires (minus the ones about clubbing a mate over the head and dragging her to my cave). That should be obvious based on what I have written. In fact, after some potential mates of mine read this book, I'm confident that I will have foolishly reduced my mating options. What was I thinking?

At least I'm honest about it. I love everything about women, minus their tendency to touch my belly button. I love their curves, the softness of their skin, and their flowery scents. I love the arch in their back, their seductive eyes, and naturally all the fun parts used in recreational procreation.

When I'm with a woman, I try to behave myself and not allow myself to be distracted. That's hard to do because you girls are so mean to each other. You'll flaunt it and try to distract me. Then I get aggravated and drink more, making it harder to remain focused. Before I realize it, my blue eyes are meeting your "brown eyes." (That's another word for nipples. Must I explain everything?) It's a vicious cycle.

Yet, I act like a gentleman. I say "act" because you all have different interpretations of that word. I try to act like the man the present woman (or women) desire. That's why I'm described as a nice guy. I have learned how to play to my audience. Sometimes the filter between my brain and my mouth dissolves, and I say or do something stupid. However, I'm also skilled at apology and recovery.

I wrote these essays almost daily over the past year. It is something that comes easily to me. I wish I could be this witty (OK, I'm presuming) in person. Instead, I'm awkwardly shy. This is going to make book signings interesting. I don't know what my problem is. I should be comfortable in front of an audience, after spending twenty years DJing. I'm comfortable, as long as people aren't paying attention to me. I prefer to lurk, observe, and report. I'm not quick-witted enough to pull off something like standup comedians do. They can be naturally funny with lightning-fast comebacks to every situation. That's a rare gift. I think of something witty to say, but it's often too late. Then I agonize over missing the opportunity.

That's why I write. I can recall the situation, embellish it, and then write about it. All I need is my handy spell-checker, thesaurus, and two cats by my side. Then I post the essay online and get to see if it's witty, silly, or boring before including it in my next book.

Nothing embarrasses me more, though, than having someone read one of my essays in front of me. I wish I had the confidence of Chef Filippi Giordano, for whom I waited tables back in my college days. He made the best food I have ever tasted (next to Mom's) and he got off on watching people eat it. He would make me dinner, put it in front of me, and anxiously watch me chew every bite. He'd grin and say, "Yes? You like? Good, huh?" I would just grunt. He had total confidence in his art; that's why he found it so rewarding.

I'm not there. When people read my essays in front of me, it scares the crap out of me. I fear the condescending raised eyebrow. I fear the "I don't get it" response. I fear the "Oh my god, how could you write that about me?" response. Why? Because I *am* a nice guy, and I really don't want to offend (or bore) anyone: at least not when I'm in arm's reach. I sometimes wish I could just isolate myself in a small cottage in Sicily with my cats and internet access. That way I could continue to toss grenades over the wall without surveying the damage. Does that sound like a nice guy to you, or a coward?

Fortunately, I received enough prodding from my friends to gather my relationship remains into a pile of words that I honestly hope got reactions out of you. Preferably those reactions include your being happy, humored, entertained, enlightened, reflective, and pensive. If I offended you, then just use your imagination and understand this was not about you. It is all about me: such a nice guy.

Made in the USA
Lexington, KY
20 November 2009